Validation Number

GW00635169

By purchasing this training manual, you have paid for the course **training m**
course certificate and **competency card**.

In order to qualify for the certificate and competency card, you need to submit the validation number below to your course tutor. The course tutor will input the number on your Candidate Result Form to ensure that you receive the course certificate and competency card that you have paid for.

It is very important that you do not lose this number. BPEC cannot issue certificates for forms that do not include the appropriate validation number.

All validation numbers are unique. Once this number has been used it will no longer be valid.

YOUR UNIQUE VALIDATION NUMBER IS:

10229362

Attach this sticker on candidate's result form

© BPEC

Contents

Module 1

Photovoltaic panels in context of renewable technologies

Module 1 – Photovoltaic panels in context of renewable technologies

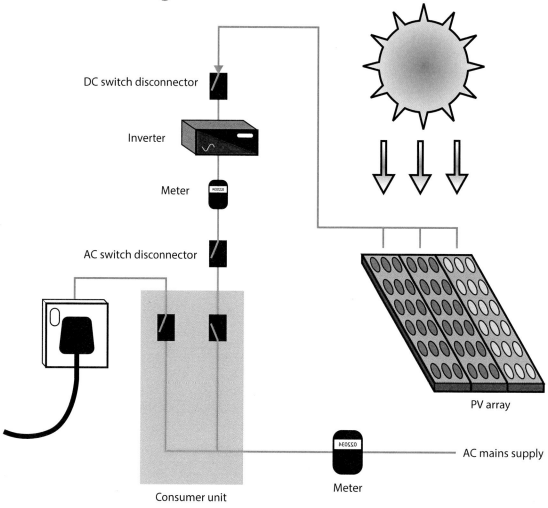

What is a PV system?

PV stands for **photovoltaic**. The definition is – *The capability of a material to produce a voltage, usually through photoemission, when exposed to radiant energy, especially light.*

The process of converting light (photons) directly to electricity (voltage) is known as photovoltaic (PV). When photovoltaic materials absorb sunlight the solar energy knocks electrons loose from their atoms, allowing the electrons to flow through the material to produce electricity. Photovoltaic material is used to build solar cells, which are usually packaged in photovoltaic modules (also known as solar panels). Modules can be grouped together and connected to form a photovoltaic array.

A PV system will incorporate a number of pieces of equipment:

● Solar panels (array)

● Mounting system

● Inverter/s (*inc. power optimisers*)

- AC/DC switch disconnector/s

- Meter

- AC/DC cabling

- Consumer unit/distribution board

Benefits of a PV system

There are different kinds of benefits to consider when looking at a PV installation. The two main benefits of PV installations are economic and environmental.

The economic benefits of a PV system are actually considered to be an investment, where a PV system requires an initial cost to install and requires very little maintenance but will continue to generate electricity, which will be purchased from the client by the Distribution Network Operator (DNO).

Below are some examples of these benefits:

Economic

- **Reduction in electricity bills**: sunlight is free, so once the initial installation is paid for, electricity costs will be greatly reduced. A typical home PV system can produce around 40% of the electricity a household uses in a year.

- **Sell electricity back to the grid**: if the system is producing more electricity than is need, or when it can't be used, someone else can use it – and the system could make a bit of money.

- **Store electricity for a cloudy day**: if the home isn't connected to the national grid, the system can store excess electricity in batteries to use when you need it.

Environmental

- **Reduction in carbon footprint**: solar electricity is a green, renewable energy and doesn't release any harmful carbon dioxide or other pollutants. A typical home PV system could save around 1200kg of carbon dioxide per year – that's around 30 tonnes over its lifetime.

- **Wildlife protection**: coal mines require large quantities of water to remove impurities from coal at the mine. At coal-fired power stations large quantities of water are used for producing steam and for cooling systems. When coal-fired power plants remove water from a lake or river, the fish and other aquatic life can be affected, as well as animals and people who depend on these aquatic resources. At the same time, pollutants build up in the water used by the power plant boiler and cooling system. If the water used in the power plant is discharged to a lake or river, the pollutants in the water can harm fish and plants. PV systems have no such processes.

- **No waste material**: The burning of coal creates solid waste, called ash, which is composed primarily of metal oxides and alkali. On average, the ash content of coal is 10%. Solid waste is also created at coalmines when coal is cleaned and at power plants when air pollutants are removed from the stack gas. Much of this waste is deposited in landfills and abandoned mines, although some amounts are now being recycled into useful products, such as cement and building materials. This is the same for nuclear-fuelled power stations, which create radioactive waste. This waste is radioactive for many thousands of years and must be stored in special locations either underground or kept in a concrete vault immersed in water or surrounded by steel. There is no exhaust or solid waste emissions from a PV system.

Disadvantages of a PV system

Below are some disadvantages of a PV system.

- Some toxic chemicals, like cadmium and arsenic, are used in the PV production process. These environmental impacts are minor and can be easily controlled through recycling and proper disposal.

- Solar energy is somewhat more expensive to produce than conventional sources of energy due in part to the cost of manufacturing PV devices and in part to the conversion efficiencies of the equipment. As the conversion efficiencies continue to increase and the manufacturing costs continue to come down, PV will become increasingly cost competitive with conventional fuels.

- Solar power is a variable energy source, with energy production dependent on the sun. Solar facilities may produce no power at all some of the time, which could lead to a shortage if a large proportion of the energy requirements are from solar power.

Types of PV systems

Photovoltaic-based systems are generally classified according to their functional and operational requirements, their component configuration, and how the equipment is connected to the other power sources and electrical loads (appliances). The two principle classifications are grid-connected and stand-alone systems.

Grid connected

Grid-connected PV systems are designed to operate in parallel with and are interconnected with the electricity grid. The primary component is the inverter. The inverter converts the DC power produced by the PV array into AC power consistent with the voltage and power quality required by the grid. The inverter automatically stops supplying power to the grid when the grid is not energised. Below is a typical grid connected PV installation.

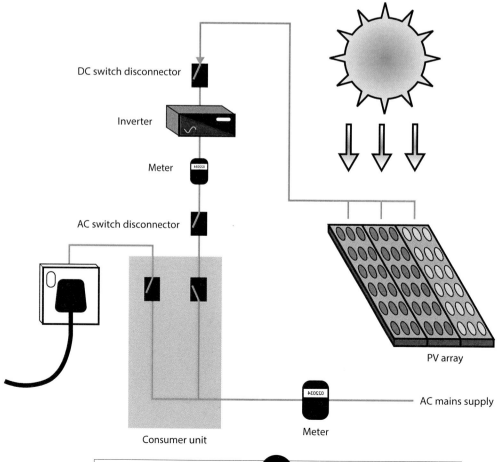

Types of PV systems

Off grid systems (stand-alone systems)

Stand-alone system

Stand-alone PV systems are designed to operate independently of the electricity grid, and are generally designed and sized to supply certain DC and/or AC electrical loads. Stand-alone systems may be powered by a PV array only, or may use wind, an engine-generator or utility power as a backup power source in what is called a PV-hybrid system. The simplest type of stand-alone PV system is a direct-coupled system, where the DC output of a PV module or array is directly connected to a DC load.

Direct - coupled stand alone system

Since there is no electrical energy storage (batteries) in direct-coupled systems, the load only operates during sunlight hours, making these designs suitable for common applications such as ventilation fans, water pumps, and small circulation pumps for solar thermal water heating systems. Matching the impedance of the electrical load to the maximum power output of the PV array is a critical part of designing well-performing direct-coupled system.

In many stand-alone PV systems, batteries are used for energy storage. Below is a diagram of a typical standalone PV system with battery storage powering DC and AC loads.

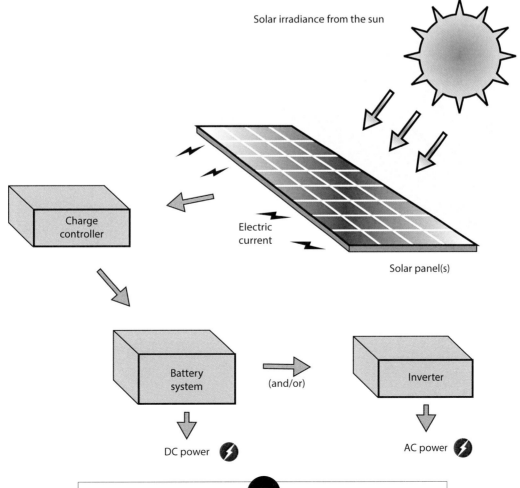

Feed-in Tariffs and ROC's

The UK Government financial incentive scheme for installation of renewables (Feed-in Tariffs) ended on 31st March 2019. Renewable Obligation Certificates (ROC's) ended on 31st March 2017.

In effect, all financial subsidies for installation of micro-renewables, solar PV included, have now been closed by the government. The result of this is customers will be required to utilise the energy they generate in order to recoup the cost of their installation.

However, the UK government are looking at an alternative arrangement for paying owners of small-scale low carbon technologies who export excess energy back to the grid. The Smart Export Guarantee (SEG) will be consulted on at the beginning of 2019 (with a closing date on the consultation being 5th March 2019). The implementation date, if the arrangement is accepted, isn't known but could be in place by the end of 2019.

Energy Storage is a new sector which would help consumers achieve self-consumption of the energy they generate but would be an additional on cost to the installation price of a solar PV system.

Costs

The cost of installing a solar electricity system can vary – an average system costs between £3000 – £7000, depending on its size and type. This includes both materials and labour charges.

In general:

- The more electricity the system can generate, the more it costs but the more it could save

- Solar tiles cost more than conventional panels

- Integrated PV roof tiles/panels are generally more expensive than non-integrated PV roof systems (retrofit systems), however, if major roof repairs are required, integrated PV roof tiles/panels can offset the cost of roof tiles.

Module 2

How a photovoltaic system works - principles and components

Module 2 – How a photovoltaic system works – principles and components

Cells, modules and arrays

Photovoltaic systems use a number of components in order to convert light energy into electrical energy. The most fundamental of these components is the cell, which we will look at first.

Cells – There are three commonly used types of cell used in the UK: Mono-Crystalline, Poly-Crystalline (also known as Multi-Crystalline) and Amorphous Silicon (also known as thin-film). These cells are made up of different materials which all have different properties. The cell with the greatest efficiency is the Mono-Crystalline cell, which has a matt black appearance. This type of cell has a 15-24% light-to-electricity conversion efficiency. Poly-Crystalline cells are blue in colour with clearly visible crystals and have an efficiency of 12-14%. Amorphous Silicon cells have an efficiency of 6-8% and are generally brown in colour. These cells have a shorter lifetime than the crystalline cells but are cheaper to buy than crystalline type due to their thinner film construction and reduction in raw materials (namely silicon). The "thin film" type of cell has the benefit of being physically thinner than the crystalline types and can be used in a greater range of applications.

PV cells operate at a low voltage, typically 0.5V for crystalline type and 0.9V for the Amorphous Silicon type. A module is a collection of cells connected in series, which will increase the voltage to make it usable in our system. A solar panel is a module, which is constructed using many cells.

Mono-Crystalline Cell

Poly-Crystalline Cell
(Image courtesy of www.szshxzy.com)

Cells, modules and arrays

Modules – A module is more commonly known as a solar panel. It consists of cells, which are electrically connected together and protected for use (hail impact, wind and snow loads). They must also protect the cells against moisture, which would corrode the metal contacts, decreasing the lifetime and performance. Most modules are rigid which would be fixed to the roofing structure of a building or a solar tracker. The electrical connections between the cells are made either in series to achieve a desired voltage output and/or in parallel to achieve the desired current output. Modules are subject manufacturing and testing compliance requirements such as British, European and International Standards. Below are the BS, BS EN and BS EN IEC codes associated with the manufacturing and testing of PV modules:

- BS EN 61215-2:2017 – Terrestrial Photovoltaic (PV) Modules. Design Qualification and Type Approval. Test Procedures

- BS EN 61215-1-3:2017 – Terrestrial Photovoltaic (PV) Modules. Design Qualification and Type Approval. Special requirements for testing of thin-film amorphous silicon based photovoltaic (PV) Modules

- BS EN IEC 61730-1:2018 – Photovoltaic (PV) Module Safety Qualification. Requirements for Construction

- BS EN IEC 61730-2:2018 – Photovoltaic (PV) Module Safety Qualification. Requirements for Testing

- MCS 005 – Product Certification Scheme Requirements: Photovoltaic Panels

IET Code of Practice for Grid Connected Solar Photovoltaic Systems should also be consulted regarding the relevant British, European and International standards which apply to modules.

Array – A photovoltaic array is an electrically linked collection of modules, which can be connected again in series or parallel depending on what value of voltage and current is required for the system. The system requirements are normally dictated by the input characteristics needed for the inverter.

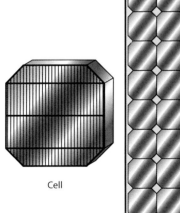

Cell

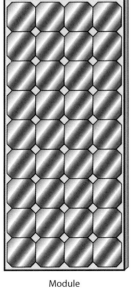

Module

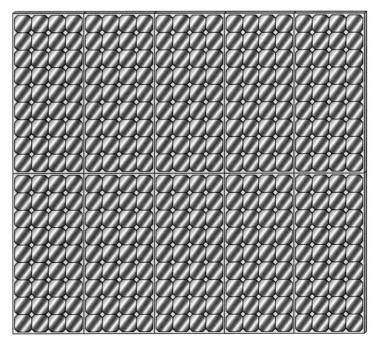

Array

Module construction

Solar modules now come in various shapes and sizes. These can vary from a solar panel to solar tiles, which would replace roof slates/tiles. Depending on which modules are installed will give different outputs. A typical crystalline solar panel, 1.6m x 1m, usually has 120 cells giving an open circuit voltage of approximately 36-40V whereas a crystalline solar tile is usually made up of between 4-6 cells and only achieves an open circuit voltage of between 2.4-3.6V. It's quite evident that the larger the area of cells, the greater power output our array will produce.

Amorphous silicon cells are different in their makeup. Instead of an actual cell arrangement, the thin film is cut into 1cm wide strips, which produce an open circuit voltage of 0.9V. These strips are then connected together to give a larger voltage output. A typical amorphous silicon module would be 3ft x 1ft but these could be constructed to be shorter which would reduce the current output or narrower, which would reduce the voltage output.

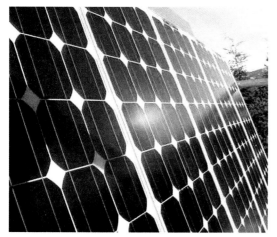

Mono-Crystalline Module
Image courtesy of www.easy-solar-power.com)

Poly-Crystalline Module
(Image courtesy of sol-energys.com/)

Amorphous Silicon Module
(Image courtesy of www.solarserver.de)

Effects of temperature, irradiance, shade and orientation on system performance

There are many characteristics to be considered when looking at modules and array configurations. The following factors will affect the efficiency of the array. All modules are rated under Standard Test conditions (STC). This is considered to be the modules maximum power output at Standard Test Conditions (STC). The STC is defined as a level of solar radiation of 1000W/m2 at a temperature of 25°C and an air mass of 1.5. This radiation and moderate temperature is an "ideal" condition for a solar module. In reality, radiation varies significantly below the peak value and the temperature is normally greater than the STC level.

In practice it may not be possible to achieve Standard Test Conditions (STC) for a number of reasons and therefore calculating the system performance is not as straightforward as first anticipated. It is crucial that system performance calculations are carried out to ensure that the yield and return from a system is accurate, or at least as accurate as possible.

There are a number of factors that affect system performance and these are discussed in the next few pages. More information on calculating system performance is provided in Module 4.

Irradiance: (sunlight intensity), this is measured in watts per metre falling on a flat surface. The measurement standard is 1000W/m2, (as above).

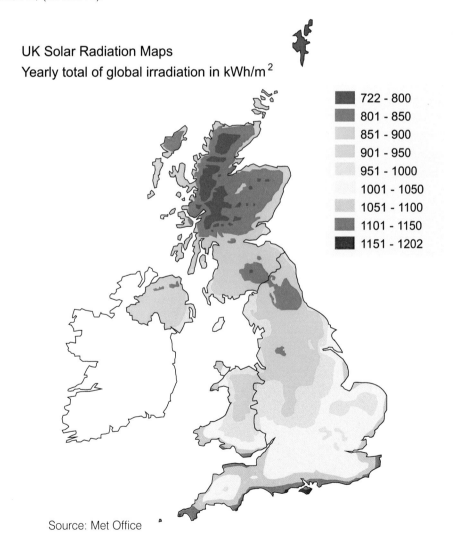

UK Solar Radiation Maps
Yearly total of global irradiation in kWh/m^2

⬛	722 - 800
⬛	801 - 850
⬛	851 - 900
⬜	901 - 950
⬜	951 - 1000
⬜	1001 - 1050
⬛	1051 - 1100
⬛	1101 - 1150
⬛	1151 - 1202

Source: Met Office

Effects of temperature, irradiance, shade and orientation on system performance

Air mass: this refers to the "thickness" and clarity of the air through which the sunlight passes to reach the modules. The sun angle will affect this value. The standard value is 1.5.

Cell temperature: this will differ from ambient air temperature. The STC value for cell testing is defined as 25°C. A PV system's efficiency reduces as the temperature increases, which in turn, has an impact on the type of mounting system to be used.

Shade: the efficiency is also affected by shading, whereby careful consideration should be given to nearby trees or adjacent buildings. This can reduce the power output of the array significantly. Therefore, the horizontal and vertical characteristics of the array can help optimise performance by reducing shading effects as well as looking aesthetically pleasing.

Shading occurs in situations where the sunlight is obscured or blocked by the surrounding environment, both built and natural, and this can have a significant effect on the PV system's performance. It is imperative that during the design consultancy stage, shading is considered as it could substantially impact on the annual yield. Typical examples of shading include surrounding building structures and trees. Temporary shading, for example, snow, bird droppings and leaves can also affect the performance of the system.

Shading reduces the level of solar irradiance which impacts on the performance of the system and careful and sympathetic design is required to ensure that shading is ideally avoided.

In a shading situation, both the current output of the shaded string is affected and thermal stress can develop in the shaded modules. Current is directly related to solar irradiance and as modules are connected in series for string configuration the output current of that string can be considerably reduced.

Reverse voltages in shaded modules can cause thermal stress. By-pass diodes block any reverse voltages in the shaded string which, considering a four string array will block any reverse voltages in the shaded string. This effectively blocks any currents that may be diverted away from the inverter and into the shaded string. The blocking state of the module and the associated losses can increase cell temperature considerably and therefore the risk of overheating is likely.

Wp is **W**att **p**eak (or the PV peak power in Watts, W, which would be produced at STC). As was discussed above, STC are rarely achievable in practice and so the Wp rating of a PV system is the potential maximum output power that a module can deliver. The actual output that the module will produce is dependent on solar radiation levels, which will vary during the day and also during the year.

Array orientation and inclination

Array orientation and inclination: the orientation of the array, that is the alignment of the array with respect to south, will have an effect on the system performance and the inclination of the surface of the modules is also a contributory factor.

The diagram below can be used as a general guide for the middle of the UK to ascertain an approximate system performance indicator based on orientation and inclination.

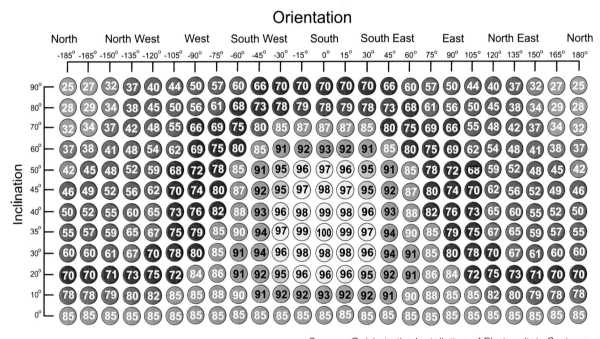

Source: Guide to the Installation of Photovoltaic Systems

From the diagram the optimum angle and inclination is 35° due South, which yields a 100% return. However, if the pitch of a South East facing roof located in the middle of the UK is 60° then the performance would be approximately 85% (or reduced by 15%).

On flat roofs, it is possible to mount PV on frames that can be angled correctly. If the PV array is to be mounted on a vertical façade the orientation should preferably be between South East and South West. North facing orientations should be avoided.

A tilted array will receive more light than a vertical array, but any angle between vertical and 15° off horizontal can be used. A minimum tilt of 15° off horizontal is recommended to allow the rain to wash dust off the array, however this may be different depending on the manufacturer. The optimal tilt angle is 30° – 40° for a south facing array in the UK, but a typical UK house roof titled at around 32° will be almost ideal. Shallower tilt angles are better for east or west facing arrays as the sun is lower in the sky as it moves away from due South. (Peak output is obtained when the plane of the array is perpendicular to the sun. Although the peak production would be obtained in Britain with an array angled at 52° at midday, to maximise output during daylight hours the tilt should be lower to average out the changing sun angle.)

Energy payback

For a well-designed **2kWp** grid connected PV system installed in the UK and located in the midlands, around **1870kWh** of electrical energy will be produced per year. A well-designed array should be installed to point **south** and angled between 30° and 40° (in our example, we've used an angle of 35°) from the horizontal for optimal performance in the UK. The estimated system performance given above has been taken from the MCS procedure. This is required for all systems installed under MCS.

A typical three-bedroom house uses **3880kWh/Year** of electricity, so a typical domestic sized PV system of **2kWp** could provide almost 50% of the total electricity requirements. This proportion would be greater in an energy efficient home of the same size, although demand may occur at a different time from generation. Installations on commercial buildings are also particularly suitable for PV, as demand for electricity occurs at the same time as generation.

(Electricity consumption of a typical three-bedroom house taken from http://www.esru.strath.ac.uk/EandE/Web_sites/01-02/RE_info/hec.htm)

The difference between AC and DC

Typical grid connected PV systems will have both DC (Direct Current) and AC (Alternating Current) configurations as part of the overall system. The output from the PV panels to inverter is DC and the resulting output from the Inverter is AC. Although DC is commonly used in electrical systems it differs greatly to that of AC. Examining a common definition of DC:

> "The movement of electrical current flows in one constant direction, as opposed to Alternating Current or AC, in which the current constantly reverses direction."
>
> Source: ENA engineering recommendation G98 (Current edition)

In essence DC is non-pulsating and maintains a consistent and direct level of current over time. This is in contrast to AC, which is pulsating and in the case of the grid supplied mains electricity the AC waveform is a sine wave. The sine wave periodically reverses direction and in addition to the amplitude of the waveform the frequency is also significant. The nominal voltage in the UK is given as 230Vrms at 50Hz. The Hertz (Hz) is a measure of cycles per second and the rms (root mean square) value differs from the peak amplitude value and is often described as a relative DC equivalent value.

Electrical characteristics

PV devices can also operate from open circuit (zero current) to a short circuit (zero voltage). It is between these two extremes that maximum power is produced – 80% of open circuit voltage for crystalline modules and 60% of open circuit voltage for amorphous silicon. This is called the **M**aximum **P**ower **P**oint.

The top of this curve indicates the Maximum Power Point of the module at 25°C.

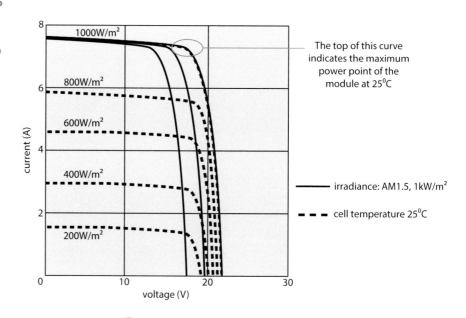

The reason behind PV modules having these current-to-voltage relationships is down to the characteristics of the cells themselves. They are made of a semi-conductive material, which has the characteristics of a diode:

- If a load of negligible impedance is applied to the system, this is essentially a short circuit. This means that the current will be at a maximum value – a short-circuit current ISC. This is the current that would flow if we were to connect the positive and negative terminals of a module together at zero voltage. (Zero power)

- If an infinite load is applied to the system, this is essentially an open circuit. This means that no current can flow and the voltage across the module will be at its maximum – this is the open circuit voltage VOC.

- When there is an applied load somewhere in between an open and a short circuit, the PV module will produce power, which will reach a maximum at the maximum power point. This is indicated on the graph above.

The diagram above shows that this cell loses voltage as the temperature increases and current as the irradiance decreases. This effect is common to all crystalline modules. The maximum power output of this cell is at the bend in the curve, a combination of a voltage value and current value.

Electrical characteristics

Inverters, which are used for grid-connected systems, have a maximum power point tracking system (MPPT), which allows the load to be managed. This helps to keep the modules/array as near as possible to the maximum power point, even through changes in the weather and electrical demands within the building. Therefore, the operating current and voltage being used by the system should be near the MPP current and voltage.

Taking some typical values from the chart on the previous page, we can see how this would affect the power output of the module.

For a temperature of 25°C and an irradiance or 1000W/M², we can calculate the power output. The voltage at the curve for these conditions is 18V and the current is 7A. We would therefore use the equation:

$$P = V \times I$$

$$P = 18 \times 7$$

$$P = \mathbf{126}W$$

This value is the maximum power we can extract from this module in ideal conditions. If the irradiance was to decrease or the temperature increase, this would have an adverse affect on our power output. For example:

1) The current at an irradiance of 800W/M² would be approximately 5.8A. If the temperature were to remain 25°C, the voltage would remain 18V. The new values would then be:

$$P = 18 \times 5.8$$

$$P = \mathbf{104.4}W$$

2) The voltage at a temperature of 50°C at an irradiance of 1000W/M2 would be 14V and the current would be 7A. This gives the following calculations:

$$P = 14 \times 7$$

$$P = \mathbf{98}W$$

It can be seen that the relationship between power output and temperature is inversely proportional, that is to say, if the temperature increases, the power output will decrease. On the other hand, the relationship between irradiance and power output is directly proportional, that is to say, if the irradiance levels increase, the power output will increase also.

Electrical characteristics

As can be seen in the examples on the previous page, it is obvious that both current and voltage are required to develop any form of power whatsoever, but what would happen if the conditions were such that the ISC or VOC were present in the system. Let's look at some examples:

1) If the conditions were such that ISC was present, then there would be a voltage of zero in the circuit. If we look at the previous diagram, we can see that the current at this point would be approximately 7.5A but the current would have a value of 0V (at STC). This would give us the following equation:

$$P = V \times I$$

$$P = 0 \times 7.5$$

$$P = \mathbf{0}W$$

2) If the conditions were such that VOC was applicable, this would result in the circuit current being zero. In the previous diagram, the VOC would be approximately 22V with a current of 0A (at STC). This gives the following equation:

$$P = V \times I$$

$$P = 22 \times 0$$

$$P = \mathbf{0}W$$

In both circumstances, the outcome is the same. If we have either an ISC or VOC value, we will produce zero power.

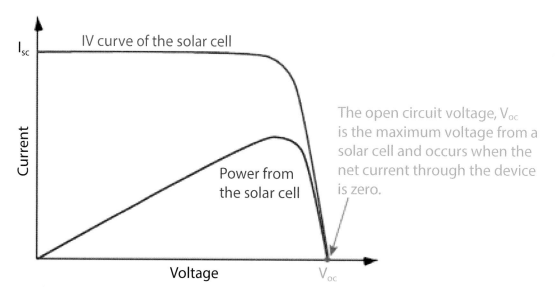

(Image courtesy of pvcdrom.pveducation.org/CELLOPER/VOC.HTM)

Electrical characteristics

There are two circumstances where certain factors can boost the current and voltage, which means that the power generated from a module, would be greater than the maximum power point indicated on the graph. The two circumstances where this could occur are **over-irradiance** and **reduced temperature**.

Over-irradiance can be caused by one of the following scenarios:

Reduced air mass: This occurs if there is a reduction in the energy-robbing atmosphere (less dust and fumes), normally at high altitude.

Edge-of-cloud effect: This situation occurs as a cloud shadow passes out of the incoming sunlight's pathway to the solar panels. Refraction, which is the change in direction of a wave due to a change in its speed, can concentrate the sunlight while the edge of the shadow passes by. This would cause a boost in the module voltage.

Ambient sunlight reflection: Nearby water and snow can reflect the sunlight causing a boost in solar intensity that can affect the voltage.

Geographic location and Time of year: The further south you go the higher the maximum irradiance with the south coast of the UK being 10-15% higher than the north. Summer time irradiance often exceeds 1000W/m^2.

Reduced temperature

Is also a key factor for increasing the energy output of a module/array. As discovered earlier, the temperature is inversely proportional to power output and this has to be taken into account when designing a PV system. The relationship between module voltage and temperature is dictated by a temperature coefficient. An example of how this can significantly affect a typical PV array is shown below.

For a system consisting of 10 series connected modules, having an open-circuit voltage of 37.5V, a temperature coefficient of -0.32%/^{o}C would be applied. This would result in the following variance in maximum voltage values from the PV array:

At STC, the PV array V_{OC} = 37.5V x 10 = 375V

At 0°C (25°C below STC), the PV array V_{OC} = 375v + (375 x 0.0032 x 25) = 405V

At -15°C (40°C below STC, the PV array V_{OC} = 375 + (375 x 0.0032 x 40) = 423V

This example shows that the array's open-circuit voltage is 48V higher at -15°C. When designing PV systems, multipliers are applied to the array characteristics to take this increase in voltage into account and suitably rate components for such increases.

Module 3

Design of a PV system

Module 3 – Design of a PV system

Series and parallel connections

The heart of PV system design relies on two basic principles, connecting modules in series increases the voltage capability and a parallel configuration yields more current capacity. This is analogous to batteries, where optimum voltage and current requirements are established by connection configurations.

Larger PV system operating voltages are achieved by connecting modules together in series (strings) to add voltages. Higher power levels are achieved by connecting strings (of equal nominal voltage) together in parallel to add currents. These properties of an array are important, as these will need to be calculated before the size of the inverter can be decided. A typical grid-connected system is illustrated below.

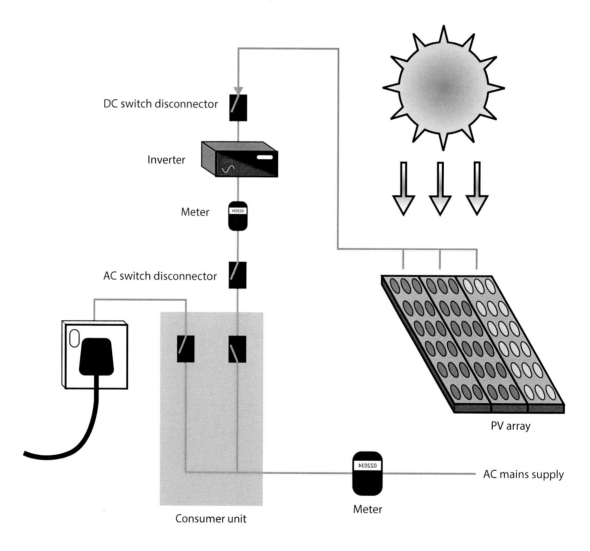

The voltage and current outputs of an array depend on the arrangement and connections of the modules. If the modules are connected in series, this will increase the overall voltage of the array. Note that there are two voltage values given to a module, one at STC and one at MPP. Take the STC output voltage of a module to be 21.0V and join 10 modules in series with each other, this gives a VOC of 210V per string. If there is a MPP voltage of 17.0V and again, the modules were connected in series, this gives a MPP voltage of 170V per string. This is a simple calculation, multiplying the voltage output of the module by the number of modules connected in series. Modules connected in series are called **strings**.

Single String Configuration: Modules in Series

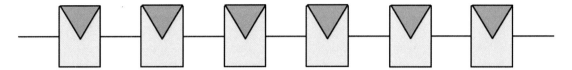

Multiple String Configuration: Modules in Series with Strings in Parallel

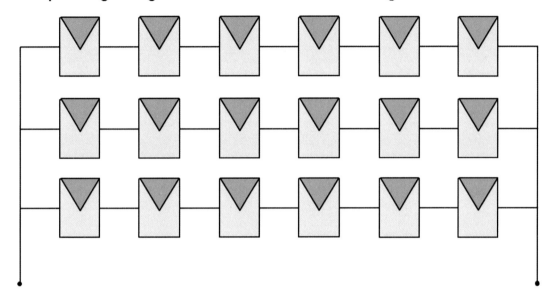

Series and parallel connections

The same process in the previous page can be used to calculate the overall current output of the array. There are also two current output values for each module, again a STC value and a MPP value. If there is a STC value of 4.75A, this value is multiplied by the number of strings in the array. If there are 2 strings of 10 modules each (a total of 20 modules), the ISC is calculated by multiplying 4.75 by 2, and this gives 9.5A for the entire array. Again, the MPP current output value of the module would also have to be calculated. If this value were to be 4.45A, this gives a MPP current output of 8.9A for the entire array.

These calculations would be laid out as below:

Array characteristics:

Open-Circuit Voltage (string) – number of modules x open-circuit voltage STC V_{OC}

MPP Voltage (string) – number of modules x VMP (Peak Power Voltage)

Array Short-Circuit Current – number of strings x short-circuit current STC ISC

Array MPP Current – number of strings x IMP (Peak Power Current)

Peak Power – V_{MP} x I_{MP}

Power Output of Array – No of Modules x Peak Power

These values are used to choose the size and specification of the inverter required for the system and will be covered in Module 4.

Example single phase layout

The diagram below illustrates a typical circuit arrangement for a single string array installed in a domestic dwelling. (The diagram is not meant to represent the schematic which should be visible at the consumer unit/ distribution board but is an example of a layout of the PV system).

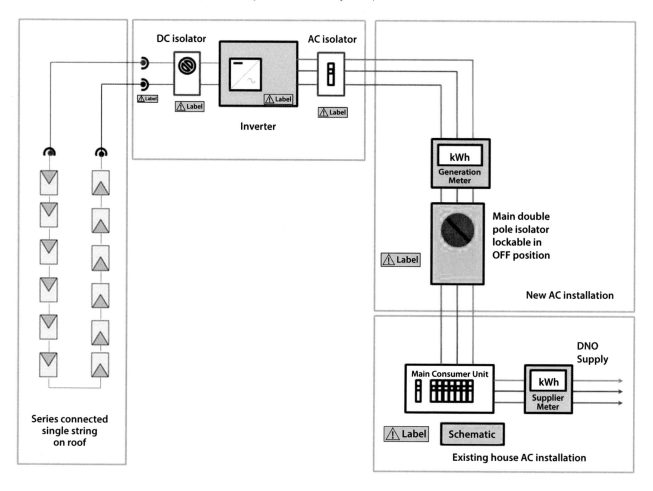

The diagram illustrates a connection to a consumers unit which are commonly found in domestic dwelling and installations up to 100A single phase. For connection to larger installations where a three distribution board is deployed, the single string array should be connected to one of the phases. The inverter is selected in accordance with Engineering Recommendation EREC G98 (current edition). An inverter selected to EREC G98 (current edition) will incorporate protection to EREC G98. In some cases inverters incorporate DC isolation and negate the requirement to provide separate DC isolation. Under no circumstances should an AC isolator be used as an alternative to a DC isolator.

Example three phase layout

The diagram below illustrates a typical circuit arrangement for a three phase two string array arrangement, connected to a three phase supply.

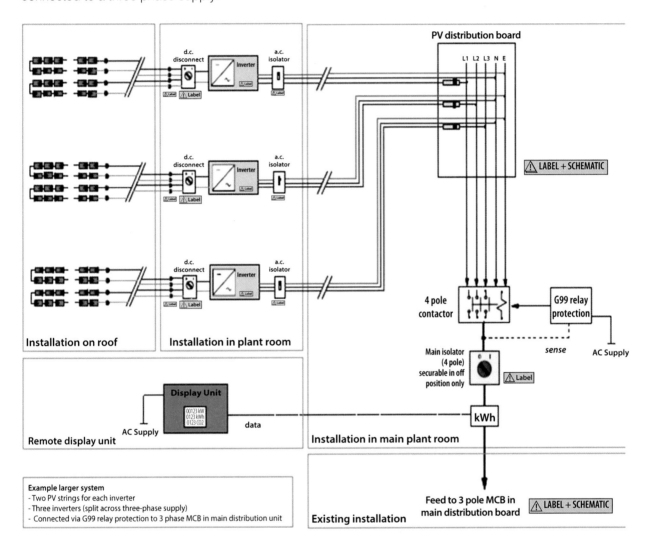

The diagram illustrates a large installation and is installed in accordance with Engineering Recommendation EREC G99 (current edition). Depending on the scale of the installation it may be possible to install a three phase installation without the requirement of the EREC G99 protection relay and this should be discussed with the DNO at the design stage before commencement of the installation which covers larger PV installations.

Care should be taken when connecting to three-phase supplies to ensure even loading of the phases.

Engineering Recommendation G59 has been replaced with Engineering Recommendation G99. Installers of systems which are included in the G99 framework should contact the relevant DNO to discuss any additional protection settings/devices required for connection to the distribution network.

Cables and connectors

This section of the module will also include a practical exercise when you attend the training course.

All DC wiring should be DC rated and completed, if possible, prior to installation of the PV array. This will allow for effective isolation of the DC system while the array is installed. This would normally require the installation of the following equipment:

- DC switch disconnector and DC junction box.

- Positive and negative cables from the DC disconnector(s)/ junction box to the either end of the PV string/array.

- PV array main cables from the DC disconnector to the inverter.

The cables used in the DC wiring system also need to be selected to ensure that they can withstand the environmental, voltage and current conditions that they will be expected to operate in. This includes the heating effects from current and sunlight.

(Image courtesy of www.santonswitchgear.com)

Connectors

The connectors for these cables should also be DC rated. BS EN 50521:2008+A1:2012 details the requirements for PV connectors. These suitably selected plugs and sockets are normally fitted between modules and strings to simplify the installation process of the array. Specific connectors, where suitable for live operation, can also provide a very good means of shock protection. Some of the characteristics to look for are:

- Connectors must be DC rated.

- Connectors must have the same or greater voltage and current ratings as the cable to which they are fitted.

- Connectors readily accessible to ordinary persons must be of the locking type (e.g. MC4), requiring a tool or two separate actions to separate, shall be labelled "Do not disconnect DC plugs and sockets under load".

- Connectors shall not and cannot be used as a form of DC electrical isolation.

- Connectors should be touch safe (i.e. to a standard of ingress protection not less than IP21), Class II, be shrouded and be of a design totally dissimilar in appearance to any connectors used for the AC system.

- Connectors that are mated together must be of the same type and same manufacturer and comply fully with BS EN 50521:2008+A1:2012

- Where "Y" connectors are used to replace junction boxes it is good practice to ensure that these connectors are in accessible locations, marked clearly on diagrams and layout drawings and labelled.

- Connectors should be compatible with the cables that they are connected to.

- Connectors should be of the same type throughout the installation unless a test report is provided confirming compatibility.

- Connectors must be UV, IP and temperature rating suitable for their intended locations.

  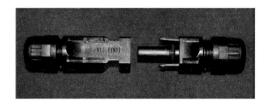

MC3 connectors
(Images courtesy of www.thepowerstore.co.uk)

MC4 connectors
(Image courtesy of Allecoenergy.com)

Calculating the ratings of the components will be covered later in this module.

All cables and conductors must be installed to comply with BS 7671 (18th Edition). Cable routes should take into consideration the potential high temperatures that can be generated on PV arrays and cables routed behind a PV array must be rated for a minimum temperature of 80°C.

Cables passing through roofs and walls should be protected from mechanical damage by the use of purpose made flashings and ducts, drilling of roof tiles, etc., and sealing with mastic **is not** acceptable.

Cables

External cables should be UV stable, water resistant, and it is recommended that they be flexible (multi-stranded) to allow for thermal/ wind movement of arrays/modules. To minimise the risk of faults, cable runs should be kept as short as practicable. Where long cable runs are required, it is good practice to label along the DC cables as follows: "Danger solar PV array cable – high voltage DC – live during daylight". This is to inform personnel involved in maintenance or alterations to a building at a later date.

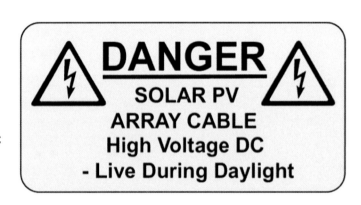

An additional DC switch may be specified for systems with long DC cable runs (typically at the point of cable entry into the building) – so as to provide a means of isolating the cable for safety reasons or maintenance works.

Labelling of DC cabling is important and for long straight runs labelling every 5 to 10 metres where a clear view between labels is possible.

There are three main types of cabling used in PV installation

● Single conductor "double insulated" cables

● Single conductor enclosed in a suitable containment system such conduit/trunking providing a sufficient degree of mechanical protection

● Single Wire Armoured (SWA) multi-core cables

The method of protection against electric shock for DC cabling is afforded by double or reinforced insulation (as per BS 7671:2018, Chapter 41). Double or reinforced insulation is an effective method providing protection against electric shock by providing two layers of insulation, or reinforced insulation between live parts and accessible parts.

Double or reinforced insulation is provided by basic insulation and fault protection is provided by supplementary insulation, or basic and fault protection are provided by reinforced insulation between live parts and accessible parts.

As a result DC cables buried in walls should be avoided as it would be difficult to identify fault or damage to the insulation which could result in shock and/or fire risk. If it is unavoidable then cables buried in walls should be installed in accordance with BS 7671:2018 Regulations 522.6.201, 522.6.202, 522.6.203 and 522.6.204.

To avoid induced voltage surges, for example lightning strikes, occurring in the PV modules, the module cables and associated DC cables should be routed with both the positive and negative cable as close together as possible. In doing so, the resultant loop formation is therefore kept to a minimum throughout the installation which limits the potential for induced voltages to occur. In areas where a high risk of lightning strikes is possible then individual shielded cables are recommended.

The potential for a serious short circuit also needs to be carefully considered with positive and negative cables routed as close together as possible, so protection from mechanical damage will need to be provided.

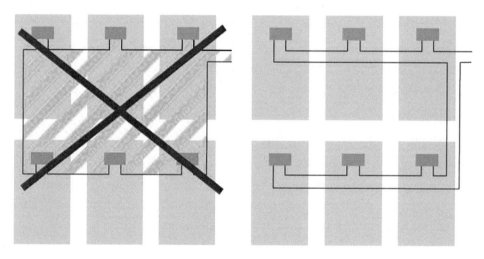

Cabling to avoid induction loops
(Courtesy of Solarpraxis)

String fuses and blocking diodes

Diodes and fuses are used in larger PV installations to prevent fire risks from overloaded cables. Typically these fuses are called string fuses, where they are connected to the main string cables, normally fitted into a DC junction box. String fuses are provided for arrays formed from four or more strings and should be fitted to both positive and negative string cables for all strings.

As the modules are current-limiting devices their short circuit will not be significantly higher than the normal current at STC. If the cables are rated for the short circuit rating and the short circuit is fixed then it is unnecessary to install string fuses for arrays that have three or fewer strings. It would simply not be able to differentiate a short circuit from a normal current. Over-sizing of cables and connectors affords better protection in this case.

For larger installations where there are more than three strings the current will be higher and the reverse current could be higher than the module series. This could lead to a risk of fire and module damage. Protection against excessive reverse currents can be achieved by the use of string fuses.

For a system of N parallel connected strings, the maximum module reverse current (IR) to be experienced under fault conditions can be determined by:

$$I_R = (N\text{-}1) \times I_{SC}$$

Overcurrent protection is required of the maximum module reverse current is greater than the module maximum series fuse rating (determined by module manufacturer as per BS EN IEC 61730-2:2018). Fuses should not be mounted where solar gains could generate a build up of heat.

String fuse selection should consider the following:

For a system of N parallel connected strings, with each formed of M series connected modules:

- String fuses must be provided for all arrays where: $(N\text{-}1) \times I_{SC}$ > module maximum series fuse rating

- Where fitted, fuses must be installed in both positive and negative string cables for all strings

- The string fuse must be of a type gV – according to BS EN 60269-6:2011

- The string fuse must be rated for an operation at V_{OC} STC x M x 1.15

- The string fuse must be selected with an operating current in such that:

    - $I_N > 1.5 \times I_{SC\_MOD}$

    - $I_N < 2.4 \times I_{SC\_MOD}$

    - $I_N \leq 1_{MOD\_MAX\_OCPR}$

    Where:

    - I_N = The rated current of an overcurrent protective device

    - I_{SC_MOD} = The module short circuit current at STC

    - $I_{MOD\_MAX\_OCPR}$ = The PV module maximum overcurrent protection rating, often termed 'maximum series fuse', as determined by IEC 61730. This expresses the ability of a PV module to cope with reverse currents

All formulae and description above are taken from IET Code of Practice for Grid Connected Solar Photovoltaic systems.

Systems with three or fewer strings in the array cannot generate sufficient fault currents to warrant the use of string fuses. This is only applicable if the string cables connected from the array to the junction box are rated for such currents. We will look at these ratings further in this module.

It should also be note that by omitting string fuses from an array of three or fewer strings, the designer of the system has verified with the manufacturer of the modules that they can withstand a reverse current of 2 x 1.15 x I_{SC} STC.

Blocking diodes

Blocking diodes are not commonly used in grid connected systems as their function is better served by use of a suitably rated string fuse. Blocking diodes prevent reverse currents flowing through parallel connected strings. Reverse currents occur where a string has failed to generate a voltage (through shading or a short circuit) and therefore supply current. Due to the string being connected in parallel, this will allow current from the other strings to pass through it in the opposite direction. This can have a detrimental effect on the modules in that string and can cause damage if the modules aren't designed for this. Blocking diodes are fitted to each string in a forward-biased direction, thus only allowing complete string currents to pass through the string.

- Blocking diodes must have:

    - a reverse voltage rating greater than 2 x maximum system voltage

    - a current rating greater than 1.4 x ISC (where ISC is the relevant short circuit current for the sting/sub array/ arrays

    - Have adequate cooling (heatsinks) if required

There are however, drawbacks to fitting blocking diodes. Due to the diode being connected in series with the string, this means that there will be a voltage dropped across it. This is approximately around 0.5V – 1V. Faulty string diodes have also proven problematic with PV strings that have completely failed not being discovered for some time.

Most grid-connected PV systems today are generally built without string diodes. Standard modules can often withstand seven times the module short-circuit current without being damaged. String diodes are not required if all of the following characteristics are met:

- If only modules of the same type are used and there less than four strings

- If they adhere to Class II protection

- Are certified to withstand 50% of the nominal short-circuit current in the direction opposite to normal current flow

- If the open-circuit voltage does not deviate by more than 5% between the array's individual strings.

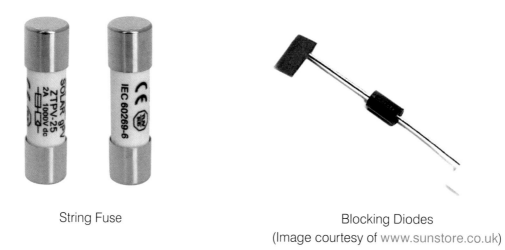

String Fuse

Blocking Diodes
(Image courtesy of www.sunstore.co.uk)

Blocking diodes should not be confused with by-pass diodes which normally form part of the module installation and used to allow currents to by-pass cells/modules that have a high resistance (normally caused by shading).

Component rating

DC component rating

All DC components (cables, switches, connectors etc) of the system must have their ratings calculated using the maximum voltages and currents of the PV array. This has to take into account the system voltages and currents of the series/parallel connected modules making up the array and also the individual module outputs. The two key values that have to be considered are the V_{OC} and I_{SC} at STC. As discussed earlier, STC doesn't occur very often in the UK but these values must be used, as there is always a possibility that these conditions could occur and our system must be able to deal with these values.

We have multiplication factors that allow for the variation that may be experienced under UK conditions for **crystalline silicon modules**.

All DC components shall be rated as a minimum for:

Voltage (V_{DC-MAX}) = V_{OC} STC x 1.15

Current (I_{DC-MAX}) = I_{SC} STC x 1.25

DC component ratings for systems fitted with power optimisers

Where modules are fitted with a power optimiser, the voltage or current output of the optimiser may be higher than that from the individual module (even after the multiplier has been applied). In such cases, the optimiser output figure becomes the relevant value to use in the design of the circuit. Therefore, the following ratings will apply:

- Voltage (V_{DC-MAX}) shall be taken as either the output of the optimiser or the value of V_{DC-MAX} as calculated previously, whichever is the greater;

- Current (I_{DC-MAX}) shall be taken as either the output of the optimiser or the value of I_{DC-MAX} as calculated previously, whichever is the greater;

Where a manufacturer can provide a written declaration that – for all possible operational and failure scenarios – the optimiser will limit its output voltage to $V_{OPT-MAX}$, then:

- For systems with a matched inverter and optimiser (from the same manufacturer): the circuit shall be rated to the inverter maximum rated input voltage; and

- For other systems (strings with M optimisers connected in series): the circuit shall be rated to : M x $V_{OPT-MAX}$

All formulae and descriptions regarding power optimisers are taken from IET Code of Practice for Grid Connected Solar Photovoltaic systems. This code of practice should be consulted when carrying out all circuit design for such systems.

Due to their differing characteristics, it is not possible to provide a simple pair of multipliers to apply to modules that are not constructed using crystalline silicon cells. For such modules installed in the UK, individual calculations need to be performed as follows:

Using manufacturer's data, the values of V_{DC-MAX} and I_{DC-MAX} shall be calculated assuming a minimum temperature of -15°C and a maximum irradiance of 1,250W/m².

DC main cables (to and from the entire array), should be rated as a minimum at:

Voltage: V_{OC} STC x M x 1.15 (where M is the number of series connected modules)

Current: I_{sc} STC x N x 1.25 (where N is the number of parallel connected strings)

DC string cables should be rated as follows:

Array with NO string fuses:

Voltage: V_{oc} STC x M x 1.15 (where M is the number of series connected modules)

Current: I_{sc} STC x (N-1) x 1.25 (where N is the number of parallel connected strings)

Array with string fuses:

Voltage: V_{oc} STC x M x 1.15 (where M is the number of series connected modules)

Current: I_{sc} STC x 1.25

In the case where there are no string fuses, the factors used for rating the cable include the value (N-1). This is derived from the theory that the maximum fault current to flow through a string cable would be N-1 x I_{sc}, where N is the number of parallel connected strings.

For smaller systems, ensure that the string cables are rated such that they can safely carry the maximum fault current. This method would rely on over-sizing the string cables such that the fault current is accommodated and although this will not clear the fault, it would prevent the risk of fire from overloaded cables.

There are also de-rating factors to be applied in accordance with BS7671:2018, appendix 4 when these are applicable. Cables also routed behind a PV array should be rated for a minimum of 80°C.

The DC cabling should also be selected to minimise the risk of earth faults and short-circuits. This can be achieved by using the following wiring methods:

- Single core cable – double insulated.

- Single core cable in suitable conduit/trunking.

- Steel Wire Armoured cable (SWA) – usually only suitable for main DC cabling.

All cables should be sized to ensure that a voltage drop of less than 3% at STC occurs between the array and the inverter. All external cables should also be UV stable, water-resistant and flexible.

AC Component rating

AC cables should be specified and installed in accordance with BS 7671. The PV system shall be installed onto a dedicated circuit that is connected to no other current-using equipment (other than any PV system data-logger or similar equipment).

AC and DC switch disconnectors

Due to the nature of a PV system, we have to incorporate both AC and DC switch disconnectors. These provide a means of manual electrical isolation of the entire PV array. These switch disconnectors are required during system installation and subsequent maintenance or repairs. These should be located adjacent to the inverter.

For DC switch disconnectors, the following should be observed:

- The DC switch must be double pole – so as to electrically isolate both the PV array positive and negative.

- The switch must be rated for DC operation.

- The DC switch disconnector shall be rated to interrupt current in either direction.

- The means of operating the DC switch disconnector shall be readily accessible and located at or adjacent to the inverter.

- The DC switch must be rated for the system voltage and current maximum.

- The DC switch disconnector shall be labelled: 'PV array DC Isolator' (or equivalent) with the ON and OFF positions clearly indicated. The enclosure shall also be labelled: 'Danger, contains live parts during daylight' (or equivalent). All labels shall be clear, easily visible, constructed and affixed to last and remain legible for as long as the enclosure.

Any DC switch disconnector installed as part of a PV system shall comply with BS EN 60947-1, Part 1 General rules and BS EN 60947-3, Part 3 Switches, disconnectors, switch-disconnectors and fuse-combination units; or where a circuit breaker is utilised, with BS EN 60947-2.

Where a system is installed using module (micro) inverters, the requirement for a DC switch disconnector at each inverter can be relaxed in certain circumstances. The omission of a DC switch disconnectors from module (micro) inverters is acceptable provided all of the following requirements are met:

- The inverter connects directly to one module;

- The inverter and the PV module interconnect directly using the factory-fitted cables and plug and socket connections (no jumper cable or modifications permitted); and

- The electrical installation certificate for the installation notes the departure from BS 7671

Equivalent AC rated switch disconnectors cannot be used for switching DC currents. AC switching is less demanding due to the value of voltage passing through 0V many times a second.

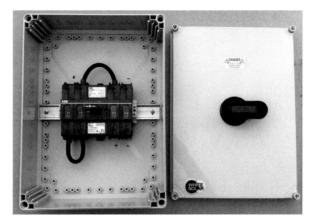

DC Switch Disconnector
(Image courtesy of www.santonswitchgear.com)

AC Isolation and Switching

For AC isolators, the following should be observed.

All grid-connected PV systems shall include a main isolation switch that:

- Isolates all inverters;

- Isolates all phase and neutral conductors to each inverter;

- Is located in an accessible location;

- Can be secured (Locked) in the off position; and

- Meets the requirements of BS 7671 section 537

AC Switch Disconnector
(Image courtesy of
www.santonswitchgear.com)

This main isolator shall be labelled 'PV system main isolator' (or equivalent).

When installing isolators in the AC circuit that feeds the inverters, cables should be connected such that the isolator terminals labelled 'supply' are connected to the cables from the mains and the terminals labelled 'load' are connected to the cables from the inverter(s).

Where an inverter is located in a different room to the main isolator, provision of a local AC isolator is recommended to facilitate maintenance of the inverter, this should be mounted adjacent to the inverter and meet the requirements of BS 7671, section 537.

DC Junction Boxes (Combiner Boxes)

DC junction boxes (also known as combiner boxes) can be used if there is more than one string. The junction box is the point where these strings are connected in parallel with one another. This would also be the point where string fuses would be connected (if applicable).

DC junction boxes should incorporate the following:

- DC junction boxes should be labelled as a 'PV array junction box', and also labelled with 'Danger, contains live parts during daylight'. All labels shall be clear, easily visible, constructed and affixed to last, and remain legible as long as the enclosure is in service.

- It is recommended that a means to disconnect and isolate individual strings from the PV array is provided. Suitable removable string fuse assemblies within the DC junction box or other removable links that can be operated safely when live can achieve this. Any such isolation should not be carried out with the system under load.

- DC junction boxes shall have an IP rating suitable for their location

The construction of the DC junction box also has to maintain the level of short-circuit protection offered from the cabling installation (BS EN 61140:2016). It is recommended that short-circuit protection is achieved by:

- Fabrication of the enclosure is completed using nonconductive materials.

- Positive and negative busbars are adequately separated and segregated within the enclosure and/or by a suitably sized insulating plate, or separate positive and negative junction boxes.

- Cable and terminal layouts should be such that short circuits during installation and subsequent maintenance are extremely unlikely.

- A junction box may also contain auxiliary circuits (e.g. a 230v supply monitoring apparatus). The design and installation of these circuits should comply with the requirements of BS 7671.

Where only two strings are to be connected, an alternative to a junction box is the string connector. Where such a connector is used to connect two string cables, it shall:

- Be rated for the voltage and current maximum, calculated for the combined circuits; and

- Meet all the requirements for the PV array and plug and socket connections, including that it shall be of the same model and from the same manufacturer as the plug/sockets it is connected to.

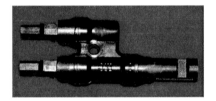
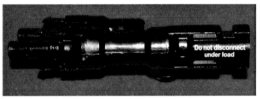

Power Optimisers

A power optimiser is a module level electrical device that conditions the output of a PV module.

Typically, the optimiser provides module-level maximum-power point tracking, with the units mounted on the rear of the PV modules or incorporated into the module junction box.

An optimiser system requires a separate inverter to enable the grid connection. There are two distinct architectures: those that are designed to work with any inverter (providing the inverter meets certain requirements), and those that are designed to work with a specific inverter (usually inverter and optimiser from the same manufacturer).

Some optimisers will work with one module each and other will work with pairs of modules. Optimisers can also provide module-level performance monitoring and additional protection features.

Safe isolation

As all PV panel are essentially live from the point of manufacture and they should therefore be considered as actually generating electricity at all time. BS 7671:2018 states that "PV equipment on the DC side shall be considered to be energised, even when the system is disconnected from the AC side" (Reg 712.410.3). This gives heightened importance to the process of safe isolation, working live in accordance with the Electricity At Work Regulations 1989 and also, sequencing of installation processes. The sequencing of installation processes needs to be carefully adhered to, ensuring that at no time during the installation the installers are exposed to potentially dangerous DC voltages. For example, glanding and terminating of cables and connectors should be carried out dead and the careful sequencing of tasks ensures protection against working with live DC tails and terminals. The sequencing of installation processes must be reflected in any risk assessment documentation to ensure appropriate dead working.

Safe Isolation is a key process in carrying out any electrical work and Solar Photovoltaic Systems are no exception. Due to the unique nature of generating the electricity, installers should perhaps have a heightened awareness of the dangers involved with the connection and maintenance of PV systems. PV systems are unusual in that they cannot be switched off, therefore, any terminals will remain live at all times during daylight hours. With this in mind, safe isolation should be used at all times to prevent electric shock and electric burns.

As good practice, the PV modules/array should be the last piece of equipment installed in the system to reduce the risks above. If this is not possible, placing a sheet or covering the array is not deemed safe isolation. The following information and procedures should be used.

The DC and AC switch disconnectors that are fitted to the PV system should be used to ensure that safe isolation can take place.

For DC isolation, the DC switch disconnector located adjacent to the inverter should be switched off (only if it has load breaking ability) to stop the DC supply reaching the inverter. In most cases, the DC switch disconnector has no function to be locked in the off position and so must have the operating handle removed and stored in a locked box which can only be accessed from the person carrying out the isolation.

For AC isolation, the AC switch disconnector located adjacent to the consumer unit shall be switched off. The AC switch disconnector shall be locked in the off position using a uniquely keyed padlock.

Caution notices should be displayed at all points of isolation, preferably giving details of the person who has carried out the isolation and how to contact them.

A set of proprietary test lamps or two pole voltage indicators (compliant with GS38) should be used at any point of the installation where work is to be carried out (providing that they are rated for both AC and DC voltages). When using voltage indicators to prove dead on the AC side of the system, the following procedure should be used:

- Voltage indicators should be proved on a known 'LIVE' source or proving unit.

- Check terminal voltages between:

  - Earth and line

  - Neutral and line

  - Earth and neutral

- Re-prove the voltage indicators on a known 'LIVE' source or proving unit.

Safe isolation

For proving dead the DC side of the system, the following procedure should be used:

- Voltage indicators should be proved on a known 'LIVE' source or proving unit.

- Check terminal voltages between:

  - Earth and positive

  - Negative and positive

  - Earth and negative

- Re-prove the voltage indicators on a known 'LIVE' source or proving unit.

PV module warranties and guarantees

Warranties for PV modules vary depending on the manufacturer. Generally, manufacturers' warranties last between 10-25 years, however, it should be noted that the warranty normally relates to a power rating. This could either be minimum power or nominal power rating. A guarantee of 90% of the minimum power with a performance tolerance of 10% is only equivalent to a guarantee of 80% of the nominal power rating.

Manufacturers' should be contacted prior to purchasing modules to clarify any warranty or guarantee issues.

Legislation

There are many different documents to be considered when installing PV systems. These include BS7671:2018 Requirements for Electrical Installations (which covers the Electricity at Work Regulations 1989), Building Regulations for Scotland, Northern Ireland, England and Wales as well as Engineering Recommendations EREC G98 (current edition) and EREC G99 (current edition).

It is advisable that the installer should either have a working knowledge or have access to these documents when designing, installing, commissioning and maintaining a PV system.

Planning permission

Permitted development rights

In England and Scotland, changes to permitted development rights for renewable technologies introduced on 6 April 2008 and 12 March 2009 respectively, have lifted the requirements for planning permission for most domestic micro-generation technologies.

The installation of Solar PV systems is permitted (without the requirements for planning permission) as long as the following requirements are met:

Always check with your local authority to find out if you require planning permission or not, this information is for guidance only.

Roof and wall mounted Solar PV (England)

Permitted unless:

- The solar PV or solar thermal equipment would protrude more than 0.2 metres beyond the plane of the wall or the roof slope when measured from the perpendicular with the external surface of the wall or roof slope;

- It would result in the highest part of the solar PV or solar thermal equipment being higher than the highest part of the roof (excluding any chimney);

- In the case of land within a conservation area or which is a World Heritage Site, the solar PV or solar thermal equipment would be installed on a wall which fronts a highway;

- The solar PV or solar thermal equipment would be installed on a site designated as a scheduled monument; or

- The solar PV or solar thermal equipment would be installed on a building within the curtilage of the dwellinghouse or block of flats if the dwellinghouse or block

Additionally, for ground mounted panels:

- In the case of the installation of stand-alone solar, the development would result in the presence within the curtilage of more than 1 stand-alone solar;

- Any part of the stand-alone solar—

   (a) would exceed 4 metres in height;

   (b) would, in the case of land within a conservation area or which is a World Heritage Site, be installed so that it is nearer to any highway which bounds the curtilage than the part of the dwellinghouse or block of flats which is nearest to that highway;

   (c) would be installed within 5 metres of the boundary of the curtilage;

   (d) would be installed within the curtilage of a listed building; or

   (e) would be installed on a site designated as a scheduled monument; or

- The surface area of the solar panels forming part of the stand-alone solar would exceed 9 square metres or any dimension of its array (including any housing) would exceed 3 metres."

Roof and wall mounted Solar PV (Scotland)

Permitted unless:

- The development would protrude more than 1 metre from the outer surface of an external wall, roof plane, roof ridge or chimney of the dwelling house;

- It would be within a conservation area.

Additionally, for buildings containing flats:

- The development would protrude more than 1 metre from the outer surface of an external wall, roof plane, roof ridge or chimney;

- It would be within a conservation area or within the curtilage of a listed building.

Additionally, for ground mounted panels:

- Any part of the development would be forward of a wall forming part of the principal elevation or side elevation where that elevation fronts a road;

- Any resulting structure would exceed 3 metres in height;

- As a result of the development the area of ground covered by development within the front or rear curtilage of the dwellinghouse (excluding the original dwellinghouse and any hard surface or deck) would exceed 50% of the area of the front or rear curtilage respectively (excluding the ground area of the original dwellinghouse and any hard surface or deck);

- It would be within a conservation area or within the curtilage of a listed building; or

- It would be development described in class 3A(1), 3C(1), 3D(1), 3E(1), 6D, 6E, 6G(1), 6H(1) or 8.

There are additional aspects to permitted development in Scotland. These can be found on the 'Guidance on Householder Permitted Development Rights'

Roof and wall mounted Solar PV (Wales)

Permitted so long as:

- Panels should not be installed above the ridgeline and should project no more than 200mm from the roof or wall surface;

- If your property is a listed building installation is likely to require an application for listed building consent, even where planning permission is not needed;

- If your property is in a conservation area, or in a World Heritage Site planning consent is required when panels are to be fitted on the principal or side elevation walls and they are visible from the highway. If panels are to be fitted to a building in your garden or grounds they should not be visible from the highway.

Additionally, for buildings with a flat roof:

- Panels cannot be sited within 1 metre of the external edge of the roof; or

- Panels cannot protrude more than 1 metre above the plane of the roof.

Additionally, for ground mounted panels:

- The panel should be sited, so far as is practicable, to minimise the effect on the amenity of the area

- Only one standalone solar panel is permitted

- No part of the installation must exceed 4 metres in height

- If the panel is within 5 metres of the boundary of the property, it cannot be more than 2 metres in height

- The panel shall not be within 5 metres of the highway

- No dimension of the panel should be greater than 3 metres

- The panel surface shall not be more than 9 square metres

Roof mounted Solar PV (Northern Ireland)

Permitted so long as:

- No part of the panel exceeds the highest part of the roof;

- No part of the panel protrudes more than 20 centimetres beyond the plane of a roof slope facing onto and visible from a road;

- Panels do not exceed the boundary of the existing roof;

- If you live in a house within a conservation area or World Heritage Site, the roof slope on which the panels are fitted must not face onto and be visible from a road.

Additionally, for buildings with a flat roof:

- Panels do not extend more than 1.5 metres above the plane of the roof;

- Panels do not exceed the boundary of the existing roof;

- If you live in a house within a conservation area or World Heritage Site, the panels must not be visible from a road.

Additionally, for wall mounted panels:

- Any part of the panel which is higher than 4 metres and closer than 3 metres to the property boundary does not protrude more than 20 centimetres from the plane of the wall.

- Panels do not exceed the boundary of the wall.

- No part of the solar panel installed on a wall of a chimney is higher than the highest part of the roof.

- If you live in a house within a conservation area or World Heritage Site the wall must not face onto and be visible from a road.

Additionally, for ground mounted panels:

- There is only one freestanding solar panel installation within the boundary of the house.

- The area of the free-standing solar panel does not exceed 14 square metres.

- No part of the panel exceeds 2 metres in height.

- No part of the panel is closer to a road than the part of the house nearest the road.

Note: The primary purpose of solar equipment must be to provide heat or energy for a domestic property. Equipment must be removed as soon as reasonably practicable when no longer in use.

Planning permission

The following are some of the installations where planning permission may be required:

- New buildings

- Listed buildings

- National Parks

- An increase in a building's volume or height

MCS and Competent Person Scheme

Regardless of the location of the installation (England and Wales, Scotland) the fundamental principles of building design and the maintenance and preservation of the integrity of buildings is essentially the same. In all cases notification to the local area building control (LABC) must be carried out. The two ways in which to do that are:

- Submitting a building notice to the LABC prior to the work commencing

- Notifying the work through a competent person scheme, which can be done after the work has been completed.

In addition to the competent person scheme, the introduction of the MCS (Micro-generation Certification Scheme) is a mark of quality and demonstrates compliance to industry standards that companies strive to meet. It highlights to consumers that companies are able to consistently install or manufacture to the highest quality every time.

In England and Wales installations would typically come under MCS and also Part P of the building regulation for Electrical Safety. In Scotland installations would typically come under MCS and the Scottish Building Standards.

Table 3.1 gives an indication of the routes for registering an installation in England and Wales.

Table 3.1 – Notification routes of installed works

Installer status			Activities that require notification	
			PV array notification	New AC circuit/installation of a generator notification
MCS Only	MCS and CPS for renewables only	MCS, CPS for renewables and Part P	Row 17 of schedule 3 of the building regulations (microgeneration)	Row 12 of schedule 3 of the building regulations (electrical)
✓			Notification must be done direct to LABC	Notification done direct to LABC unless installer uses a Part P registered subcontractor
	✓		Notification made through competent persons scheme for row 17 (microgeneration)	Notification done direct to LABC unless installer uses a Part P registered subcontractor
		✓	Notification made through competent persons scheme for row 17 (microgeneration)	Notification made through competent persons scheme for row 12

Notes:
1. A full list of Competent Person Scheme (CPS) providers can be found on the CLG website at:
   http://www.communities.gov.uk/planningandbuilding/buildingregulations/competentpersonsschemes/
   existingcompetentperson/

Building regulations

The building regulations relating to projects in England and Wales are covered by Approved Documents to the Building Regulations, whereas in Scotland they are covered by the SBSA (Scottish Building Standards Agency).

Generally in England and Wales the following parts of the building regulations will apply:

- Part A – **Structure**; depth of chases in walls, and size of holes and notches in floor and wall joists.

- Part B – **Fire Safety**; fire safety of certain electrical installations; provision of fire alarm and fire detection systems; fire resistance of penetrations through external walls.

- Part C – **Site Preparation and Resistance to Moisture**; moisture resistance of cable penetrations through walls and floors.

- Part E – **Resistance to the Passage of Sound**; penetrations through walls and floors should not allow the transmission of sound between rooms/floor levels.

- Part F – **Ventilation**; means of ensuring ventilation systems are not obstructed and are capable of providing adequate means of ventilation for people in the building.

- Part L – **Conservation of Fuel and Power**; energy efficient lighting; reduced current-carrying capacity of cables in insulation.

- Part M – **Access to and Use of Buildings**; height of socket outlets, switches and consumer units.

- Part P – **Electrical Safety**; system installation, inspection and testing, commissioning and certification of work, competency of installers.

In Scotland, the regulations are split into six sections. These are:

- Structure

- Fire

- Environment

- Safety

- Noise

- Energy

There may not be as many sections as in England and Wales but the requirements and responsibilities on the installer are the same. The exception is Part P, in Scotland any work on the fixed wiring of a property **MUST** be completed by a qualified electrician.

In all cases, the following areas should be considered:

- Assessment of the strength of supporting structure and fixing method of modules.

- Compliance with fire regulations with specific attention paid to the PV modules and cabling, particularly where they pass through fire barriers.

- Some form of weatherproof membrane (e.g. roofing felt) must be installed underneath the modules that are integrated into the roof and weatherproofing of cable entries through roofs and walls etc.

- Accessibility of switches and isolators.

- Wind loading should be assessed.

- Installation by competent persons with compliance with BS 7671 and EREC G98.

- Compliance with Permitted Development Rights and environmental impact regulations.

However, you should make sure that you have copies or access to copies of the building regulations/standards to refer to for specific requirements for jobs you are carrying out. Building regulations approval and/or planning permission may be specifically required for roof-integrated systems and new build projects.

The Electricity at Work (EAW) Regulations 1989

The Electricity at Work Regulations passed through Parliament in 1989 and came into force on 1 April 1990. Their purpose is to require precautions to be taken against the risk of death or personal injury from electricity in work activities. The Regulations were made under the Health and Safety at Work Act 1974, which imposes duties on employers, employees and the self-employed.

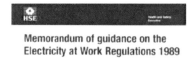

Memorandum of guidance on the Electricity at Work Regulations 1989

These Regulations (EAW) are more specific and concentrate on work activities at or near electrical equipment and make one person primarily responsible to ensure compliance in respect of systems, electrical equipment and conductors; this person is referred to as the 'duty holder'. They were also designed to include all the systems that BS 7671:2018 does not cover, such as voltages above 1000 volts AC.

There are 33 regulations and 3 appendices within EAW 1989 but not all of them apply to all situations. This section contains an overall look at the relevant regulations and what they mean to give you an appreciation of what they are about. For detailed information read 'The memorandum of guidance on Electricity at Work Regulations 1989'.

Regulation 3 deals with duty holders and the requirement imposed on them by these regulations.

There are three categories of duty holder, namely:

- employers

- employees

- self-employed persons.

The duty holder is the person who has a duty to comply with these regulations because they are relevant to the circumstances within their control. Such a person must be competent.

Whenever a regulation does not use the phrase 'so far as is reasonably practicable' this means it is an absolute duty, i.e. it must be done regardless of cost or any other consideration.

Whenever a regulation does use the phrase 'as far as is reasonably practicable' this means that the duty holder must assess the magnitude of the risks against the costs in terms of physical difficulty, time, trouble and expense involved in minimising that risk(s).

The onus is on the duty holder to prove in a court of law that he or she took all steps as far as is reasonably practicable.

Regulation 5 has four parts. This regulation states that 'no electrical equipment must be used where its strength and capability may be exceeded and give rise to danger', for example, switchgear should be capable of handling fault currents as well as normal load currents, correct size cable etc.

An example is the installation of a socket near the back door of a house. There may be nothing plugged into it at present but it is reasonable to assume that it could be used in the future for plugging in an appliance to be used outside, such as a lawnmower, which would therefore necessitate protection by an RCD. This is an absolute duty.

Regulation 7 is concerned with conductors in a system and whether they present a danger to persons. All conductors must either be suitably covered with insulating material and protected, or if not insulated (such as overhead power lines), placed out of reach 'as far as is reasonably practicable'.

Regulation 8 deals with the requirements for earthing or other such suitable precautions that are needed to reduce the risk of electric shock when a conductor (other than a circuit conductor) becomes live under fault conditions. This consists of such things as earthing the outer conductive parts of electrical equipment that can be touched and other conductive metalwork in the vicinity such as water and gas pipes. Other methods of protection could include use of reduced voltage systems, double insulated equipment and RCDs. This is an absolute regulation.

Regulation 10 requires that all joints and connections in a system must be mechanically and electrically suitable for its use. For example things like taped joints on extension leads are not allowed. This is an absolute regulation.

BS 7671:2018 Requirements for Electrical Installations (IET Wiring Regulations 18th Edition)

BS 7671:2018, sometimes referred to as the wiring regs, cover all electrical installations which supply up to 1000 volts. The document represents the main guidelines for all practical applications involved in the electrical industry and is justifiably known as the 'electrician's bible'.

BS 7671:2018 Requirements for Electrical Installations (IET Wiring Regulations 17th Edition) is a British Standard and is published by the Institute of Engineering and Technology (IET). The IET were formally known as the Institute of Electrical Engineers (IEE) and merged some years ago to form the IET. However, it has only recently dropped the IEE logo from the publication, such was the popularity and brand association of the document. It is often referred to as the 17th Edition although since its incorporation as a British Standard this is now a sub text within the title.

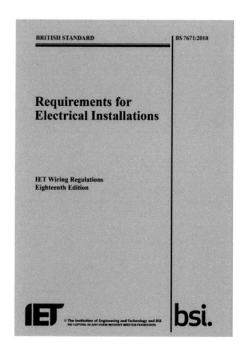

BS 7671:2018 Requirements for Electrical Installations represent an all encompassing set of documents that give both technical and practical guidance on the installation and maintenance of electrical services. Whilst not being embedded in an act of parliament (i.e. so compliance with them is not actually the law of the land), the Wiring Regulations do have sufficient authority to make it all but impossible to legally install electrical services that do not comply with them. In Scotland compliance with these Regulations is a requirement of the Building Standards and is therefore a legal requirement.

A section contained within the Special Installations or Locations relates directly to Solar PV systems, **Section 712 – Solar Photovoltaic (PV) Power Supply Systems**. This section only takes into consideration grid connected systems, stand-alone systems are under consideration by the IET.

The Regulations are in seven parts as follows:

- **Part 1** Scope, objects and fundamental principles

- **Part 2** Definitions

- **Part 3** Assessment of general characteristics

- **Part 4** Protection for safety

- **Part 5** Selection and erection of equipment

- **Part 6** Inspection and testing

- **Part 7** Special installations or locations

There are 17 appendices included in BS7671:2018. These all contain supplementary information for the first 7 parts of the regulations including appendix 4 which relates to cable selection including shock protection, volt drop and thermal constraints calculations.

Copies of BS 7671:2018 Requirements for Electrical Installations can be obtained from the Institution of Engineering and Technology (www.theiet.org.uk – formally the Institution of Electrical Engineering – IEE)) or from the British Standards Institution (www.bsi.org.uk). Again, it's recommended you try to become familiar with this document as it is an essential reference resource.

The following section deals with some of the requirements of these regulations and how they impact upon the installation of electrical systems in domestic properties.

IET Guidance Notes

As well as the full requirements (BS 7671:2018) and the On-Site Guide, the IET publish a series of eight different guidance notes.

GN1: Selection and Erection of Equipment, 8th Edition

GN2: Switching and Isolations, 8th Edition

GN3: Inspection and Testing, 8th Edition

GN4: Protection Against Fire, 8th Edition

GN5: Protection Against Electric Shock, 8th Edition

GN6: Protection Against Overcurrent, 8th Edition

GN7: Special locations, 6th Edition

GN8: Earthing and Bonding, 7th Edition

It is useful to know what these cover, but a full exploration of most of these documents falls outside the requirements of this training package.

Labelling and isolation of defective equipment (Guidance Note 3)

The following guidelines refer to the labelling and isolation procedures for defective equipment and appear in Guidance Note 3 – Inspection and Testing.

Suitable warning notices, suitably located are required to be installed to give warning of:

Voltage

- Where nominal voltage exceeding 230 volts exists within an item of equipment or enclosure and where the presence of such a voltage would not normally be expected.

- Where a nominal voltage exceeding 230 volts exists between simultaneously accessible terminals or other fixed live parts.

- Where different nominal voltages exist.

Isolation

- Where live parts are not capable of being isolated by a single device

IET On-Site Guide to the Wiring Regulations

BS 7671:2018 is a complex document to understand. The IET produce another smaller document called the On-Site Guide for competent electricians to use on a day-to-day basis instead of carrying around the full Wiring Regulations.

On-Site Guide, BS 7671:2018

The On-Site Guide covers the following types of electrical installation:

a) Domestic installations generally, including off peak supplies and supplies to associated garages, outbuildings and the like.

b) Industrial and commercial single and three phase installations where the distribution board(s) or consumer unit is located at or near the supplier's cut out.

IET Electricians Guide to the Building Regulations

This publication gives guidance on Part P of the Building Regulations for England and Wales and on other parts of the Building Regulations that persons carrying out electrical installations will be expected to comply with.

The guidance contained in the document is designed to provide information to meet:

- The competence requirements for a Principal Duty Holder and a Qualified Supervisor as required by Electrotechnical Assessment Scheme (EAS) Minimum Technical Competence of Enterprises (Level A) that undertake electrical installation work in dwellings

- The competence requirements for a Level B operative for a limited scope (non-electrotechnical) enterprise defined in Part B of the Electrotechnical Assessment Scheme (EAS) Minimum Technical Competence of Enterprises

Engineering Recommendations

There are two engineering recommendations that should be consulted when designing a PV system. These are:

- Engineering Recommendation EREC G98 (current edition)

- Engineering Recommendation EREC G99 (current edition)

G98 'Requirements for the connection of Fully Type Tested Micro-generators (up to and including 16A per phase) in parallel with public Low Voltage Distribution on or after 27th April 2019'. Under G98, the installer is required to inform the DNO on the day of connection and then provide full details within 28 days.

G99 'Requirements for the connection of generation equipment in parallel with public distribution networks on or after 27th April 2019'. This engineering recommendation relates to PV systems **over 16 amps per phase'.**

A list of DNO can be found on the following webpage:

http://www.nationalgrid.com/uk/Electricity/AboutElectricity/DistributionCompanies/

DNO approval

Grid connected PV installations are essentially generators connected in parallel and as a result, dependant on installation size, fall under either Engineering Recommendations EREC G98 (current edition) and EREC G99 (current edition), published by Energy Networks Association (ENA). Whilst these recommendations cover all types of generators that are connected in parallel there is considerable guidance on the connection process and arrangements for PV installations.

The following information offers a summary on the application process for connection to DNO networks. Electrical Networks Association has comprehensive guides on the connection process for micro-generators. The summaries given below do not relate to installations containing energy storage equipment.

Installations installed under EREC G98:

Connection Process 1: Installation of one or more distributed generation units at a single premises ≤16A/Phase using G98 Fully Type Tested Equipment;

- Installer must submit the "Installation Commissioning Confirmation" form to the DNO **within 28 days of commissioning**. DNO's may have their own forms.

Connection Process 2: Installation of distributed generation units at more than one premises within a close geographic region (normally within 500m or the same postcode with the exception of the last two letters) ≤16A/Phase using G98 Fully Type Tested Equipment;

- Installer to exchange information with DNO regarding the project,

- Installer to submit application form to DNO (this may be DNO specific),

- Installer to receive acceptance from DNO in the form of a connection offer,

- Installer must submit the "Installation Commissioning Confirmation" form to the DNO for each premises **within 28 days of commissioning**. DNO's may have their own forms.

Installations installed under EREC G99:

Connection Process 3: Installation of Type A Power Generating Modules where the registered capacity is > 16A/Phase but less than 1MW and the connection point is below 110kV;

- Installer to exchange information with DNO regarding the project,

- Installer to submit application form to DNO (this may be DNO specific),

- Installer to receive acceptance from DNO in the form of a connection offer,

- Installer to submit relevant compliance forms (Fully Type Tested or on-site testing),

- Installer must submit the relevant commissioning forms to the DNO **28 days prior to commissioning**. These forms would include information on the installation and the full results of the commissioning tests.

Connection Process 4: Installation of Types B-D Power Generating Modules where the registered capacity is > 1MW and/or the connection point exceeds 110kV;

- Project Planning Phase. Formulation of plans for the project and consulting published information to identify opportunities for connection to the network,

- Information Phase. Exchanging information with the DNO regarding the project and discussion over the issues and costs involved,

- Design Phase. Submission of a formal connection application. DNO prepares the connection design and issues a Connection Offer which includes detailed connection designs and costings,

- Construction Phase. Enter into a contract with the DNO. Either the DNO, an ICP (Independent Connections Provider) or a combination of the two construct the connection infrastructure. Submission of a draft Power Generating Module Document (PGMD),

- Notification (For Type D installations only). An Energisation Operational Notification (EON) and an Interim Operational Notification (ION) is obtained,

- Compliance, Testing and Commissioning Phase. Completion of necessary agreements with DNO. Testing and commissioning of the Power Generation Facility – where the DNO may wish to witness this. Submission of commissioning forms and other relevant data, including a completed PGMD. The DNO issues Final Operational Notifications (FON).

The following are definitions of the different types of installation under EREC G99:

Type A – Power Generating Modules where the registered capacity is > 16A/Phase but less than 1MW and the connection point is below 110kV,

Type B – Power Generating Modules where the registered capacity is > 1MW but < 10MW and the connection point < 110kV,

Type C – Power Generating Modules where the registered capacity is > 10MW but < 50MW and the connection point is < 110kV,

Type D – Power Generating Modules where the registered capacity > 50MW and/or the connection point exceeds 110kV.

Engineering Recommendations

In addition to compliance with BS 7671, EREC G98/1 states that the following requirements need to be met for grid connected PV inverters:

Inverter Interface Protection settings:

- Anti-islanding*/loss-of-mains protection

- Minimum reconnection time of 20s after supply has been restored,

- Operate at a power factor within the range of 0.95 lagging to 0.95 leading, relative to the voltage waveform,

- Limits for operating voltage and operating frequency are:

Table 3.2 – Interface protection settings for G98 installed inverters in the UK

Protection function	Trip setting	Time delay setting
Under-Voltage	230V – 20% = 184V	2.5s
Over-Voltage (Stage 1)	230V + 14% = 262.2V	1.0s
Over-Voltage (Stage 2)	230V + 19% = 273.7V	0.5s
Under-Frequency (Stage 1)	47.5Hz 20s	20s
Under-Frequency (Stage 2)	47Hz 0.5s	0.5s
Over-Frequency 52Hz	0.5s	0.5s
LoM (RoCoF)	1.0Hzs^{-1}	

Interface protection settings table – Courtesy of EREC G98

Additional settings in relation to EREC G98 are also incorporated in type tested inverters. These settings can be viewed by downloading a copy of EREC G98.

*Islanding is the phenomenon whereby a section of the distribution network which has otherwise been disconnected or isolated from the main supply has become live i.e. an isolated section of the network is said to be islanded if it is live due to an independent connected generator.

This is of great concern to network maintenance personnel where normal working practice is to assume that as the main connection has been isolated and the cables are not live. This dictates that any independent connected generator is not permitted to sustain operation when the mains network is lost.

Safety and fire regulations

The following safety and fire regulations must be complied with:

- Health and Safety at Work Act 1974

- Electricity at Work Regulations 1989

- Manual Handling Operations Regulations 1992 (as amended in 2002)

- Control of Asbestos at Work Regulations 2002

- Control of Substances Hazardous to Health Regulations 2002

- CDM (Construction, Design and Management) Regulations 2015

- BS476 Part 3 – External Fire Exposure test will give a rating to a type of PV system/mounting:

  - For roof coverings relating to the spread of fire between buildings

  - Restricts how close a roof covering can be installed relative to other buildings

  - Restriction in covering party walls in a larger building

Particular attention should be paid to the CDM 2015 regulations. These regulations stipulate:

- A health and safety plan is required

- A health and safety file is required

- The planning, detailed design, tendering, construction and commissioning of works be documented

- The handover (including the operation and maintenance) of the works should be documented

- Identify the responsibilities of the client, designer, installer and facility manager/maintainer

- The CDM 2015 Regulations **DO NOT APPLY** to construction projects lasting 30 days or less which involve 500 or less work days and employ less than five people on site unless demolition or dismantling is involved.

- The CDM 2015 Regulations **DO NOT APPLY** to work carried out by a contractor working directly for a private householder on their own residence.

Regulations

The following documents cover the legal requirements relating to grid connected PV systems in buildings and should be referred to for further information:

- Engineering Recommendation G98 (current edition)

- Engineering Recommendation G99 (current edition)

- Electricity at Work Regulations – 1989

- BS 7671:2018 Requirements for Electrical Installations (IET Wiring Regulations 18th Edition)

- Health and Safety at Work Act – 1974

- Control of Substances Hazardous to Health Regulations (COSHH) 2002

- Construction (Design and Management) Regulations 2015

- Electricity Safety, Quality and Continuity Regulations – 2002

- Health and Safety (Safety Signs and Signals) Regulations 1996

Engineering Recommendations can be purchased from the ENA website: https://shop.bsigroup.com

All British Standards publications can be purchased from the BSI website: http://bsonline.techindex.co.uk/

Code of Practice

The IET have developed a code of practice (IET Code of Practice for Grid Connected Solar Photovoltaic Systems) which provides further information relating to the design and application of grid-connected PV systems in buildings. They have also developed a code of practice for electrical energy storage systems which provides additional information on the design and installation of battery storage solutions.

Module 4

Installation of a PV system

Module 4 – Installation of a PV system

Installation of PV modules
(Image courtesy of www.feranova.com)

Fundamental design principles

Before designing a solar photovoltaic array for a client, the characteristics of the building have to be assessed to decide whether a PV system is suitable for installation. These would include the following:

● Does the building have a suitable roof/façade structure that would support the load of a solar photovoltaic array? A survey of the load bearing capability of the structure would be recommended before design work would be carried out.

● Does the building have a large enough roof/façade space at the correct angle (typically between 30° – 40°) to allow the installation of a cost effective solar photovoltaic array to be installed? This is an important aspect of the installation information required as this will determine if the PV installation would be cost effective for the client and would directly affect the number of modules/solar irradiation values which would affect the array output.

● Does the building have a south facing roof/façade which the solar photovoltaic array can be mounted to? If the building does not have a south facing roof/façade, this would reduce the amount of solar irradiation that the array would be exposed to which would reduce the output of the array.

● Which materials have been used to construct the building and can a solar photovoltaic array be suitably affixed to these materials? If, for example, there is a sloped roof using roof trusses, this may allow the fixing of roof hooks and a bracket system whereas a different type of system would be required for a flat concrete roof, possibly a secondary frame installation may need to be installed. There may also be certain circumstances where a solar photovoltaic array cannot be installed.

Before starting work

Planning to install

Starting planning work in a comfortable home or desk environment ahead of arriving on site can be a productive activity. Based on the site survey and system specification, you should be able to do the following resource planning:

- Draw up a timeline or schedule of work (including subtasks) for the installation.

- List all the parts: those which are available and those which yet to be obtained, having already checked on delivery that all delivered equipment is complete and undamaged.

- List all the documentation, tools and equipment including safety and access equipment required for the particular job.

- Decide how many skills, people and hours are likely to be needed, schedule their work diaries accordingly.

- List all the required pre-site activities such as informing regulators, reconfirming residents parking, sanitation provision, water supply, power supply arrangements, that the client will be available when you arrive and sometimes a sequential list of parts, suppliers where commonly available parts can be picked up on the way to site.

- Sort and pack the required tools and equipment into three groups of containers: roof work, inside work and generic.

- Close to the date arrange travel, select a vehicle if necessary and plan a route bearing in mind the weather and road conditions and the possible need to collect common parts en route.

The MCS, as part of their inspection, will require evidence within the company of a formalised system that documents the realisation of what they term the 'installation and set to work' phase of the installation.

Simple project planning tools exist that can help provide a timeline for the whole process as well as identify intermediary target dates to manage progress along the way. Perhaps the most suitable of these tools is the Gantt chart that can be generated from a computer programme and easily modified to cope with the inevitable changes in the plan.

Important elements of the Gantt chart may include:

Planning consent being gained. Assuming planning permission (if not 'permitted development') has been applied for and granted, then deposits or part payments and contracts can be agreed with the customer.

Building control notification. This must be given and the appropriate details provided from the system specification and plan.

Suitable risk assessments. The risk assessments and method statements covered in the last chapter must be applied to the specific job, with any variations recorded.

Tentative installation date. Once a tentative installation date has been identified and the parts required from the system specification ordered, final site access, storage locations and pipe-routing and working schedules can be determined.

Confirmed installation date. When the date agreed with the customer for the installation comes around, then access to the roof and internal working areas, storage for the system components and the implementation of site health and safety procedures will need to be finalised and implemented.

Delivery of the equipment. If delivery is to the customer, this must be organised and checks made to ensure that no damage or omissions have occurred.

Duration of installation. Installation of a system usually requires at least two days for a retrofit system with a two person team.

Pre-installation checks

Based on the site survey and design specification, the following pre-installation checks should be performed as to the:

- Suitability of the proposed location and position of the solar modules for optimum collection capacity

- Suitability of the building structure and the building fabric in relation to the installation of the system components

- Verification that the generation capacity of the proposed installation is appropriate to the property

- Inspection of existing electrical input service

- Proposed siting of key internal system components

Summary of sequencing of on-site subtasks

All DC wiring should if possible be completed prior to installing a solar photovoltaic array. This will allow effective electrical isolation of the DC system (via the DC switch-disconnector and PV module cable connectors) while the array is installed; and effective electrical isolation of the PV array while the inverter is installed. Typically this would require an installation of:

- DC switch-disconnector and DC junction box(es)

- String/array positive and negative cables – from the DC switch-disconnector/junction box to either end of the PV string/array

- PV array main cables from DC switch-disconnector to the inverter.

This should be carried out in such a way that it should never be necessary for an installer to work in any enclosure or situation featuring simultaneously accessible live PV string positive and negative parts. While the installer will be handling live cables during the subsequent module installation, because the circuit is broken at the DC switch-disconnector, there is no possibility of an electric shock current flowing from the partially completed PV string. The maximum electric shock voltage that should ever be encountered is that of one individual PV module. Where it is not possible to pre-install a DC switch-disconnector (for example, a new-build project where a PV array is installed prior to the plant room being completed), cable ends/connectors should be placed temporarily into an isolation box and suitably labelled.

External roof access and roof work

To cause minimum disruption to the household, and to reduce possible impact of weather related delays, all exterior work including roof access and roof-work should normally be tackled first. This may cause problems where an array is then live and generating. In this situation it should be terminated in an enclosure within the property ready for connection to the DC cabling when the rest of the installation is complete. If this is not practical then the roof work and installation of the array should be the last task to be completed.

Internal work

This can usually be done at the same time as the roof work if safety considerations permit. Weather may sometimes force internal to happen first.

It is usual that the inverter, DC and AC switch disconnectors and export meter are installed first and then cabling between them is installed.

Tools required (depending upon actual site/job requirements)

All on-site electrical equipment shall be low voltage battery operated under 36 volts DC or 110 volts AC provided by an approved mains transformer or generator supply. Electrical equipment must not be used in damp or wet conditions. All non-cordless electrical equipment must be PAT tested.

3 way combination step ladder

3 x 3.5m ladder   7.2m extended

4.3m extending roof ladder   7.6m extended

2.9m extending roof ladder   4.6m extended

2 roof buckets of different colours if possible (with angled base approximately 30°)

Harness + 1.5m lanyard

Hand jammer (ascension)

Rope – 10-12mm thick x 30m long (adequate for fall arrest)

Detachable rope cover 1m for protection at ridge

Tool belt

Indelible marker/pencil

Chalk (for marking out)

Kneeling/walking boards (to span joists in loft – approximately 1.2m x 0.5m)

Dust sheets (from door to loft – approximately 20m)

Tape measure – 5m

Mastic gun for silicone sealant

Combination spanners – 10, 13, 17, 19mm   12" adjustable up to 34mm

Sockets + wrench – 10, 13, 17, 19mm

Screwdrivers – flat, posidrive, Phillips (various sizes), terminal

Stanley knife + blades (retractable)

Wood saw – suitable for joists

Wire brush

Spirit level (pocket size)

Hacksaw – 300mm + 24t blades

Claw hammer

4.5" Grinder, cutting discs (for roof tiles)

Drill SDS with adapter chuck – 110v + 2m extension or minimum 24v cordless

Drill bits   wood flat up to 16mm

metal various up to 13mm

masonry, SDS 5.5, 6, 8, 10, 16mm 160mm long, 6mm 210mm long

10, 16mm 450mm long (walls)

22mm diamond tipped drill bit

Roll of lead flashing – 300mm wide

0.5 tube of silicone sealant – roof grade low modulus (e.g. Dow Corning 791 black or clear)

Electrical PVC Insulation tape – brown + blue for marking line and neutral

Wire cutters

Pliers

Test meters complying with GS38

DC and AC cables

MC3 and MC4 assembly tools

Crimp tools and fittings

Inspection Lights with clips

Portable headlamp light

Hand held digital thermometer (range 0-200°C)

Magnetic compass with flat edge or GPS

Overalls

Dust mask

Safety boots

Gloves insulating and chemical proof

Dust mask, hard hat, waterproofs

Tissues and wipes

First aid kit

A minimum of two competent people are required at all times.

All materials used shall be specified by the system manufacturer and used/installed in line with manufacturer's instructions.

Where necessary a COSHH assessment will be undertaken and all operatives instructed in and supplied with relevant information on safe methods of use and storage.

The journey to and from site

Before starting, carry out a weather-risk assessment.

On loading the van, note all relevant serial numbers of equipment.

Regarding long journeys to site, maybe:

- Consider safety and tiredness and breaks

- Take a short refreshment break shortly before arrival, and call the client at this point about your arrival time.

- In transit, all goods and equipment should be securely stored in vehicles in order to minimise the possibility of damage or theft.

On arriving at site

- Check that all goods and equipment are undamaged.

- Secure the vehicle.

- Identify and introduce yourselves initially to the customer, saying you will reassess the site and that you plan to meet them again before you start work.

- Repeat the weather-risk assessment. Postpone the roof work if unsafe.

- Examine the site conditions fully for all other aspects of health and safety.

- Examine the condition of the roof and photograph it in detail. Make the customer aware of any damage such as broken tiles – before any work has started.

- Check installation feasibility and the accuracy of all earlier surveys including checking proposed panel elevation, pitches and also orientations using a compass with corrections for magnetic deviation.

- Also check inside the property to determine if the loft is safe and free from obstruction.

- Check all intended cable routes and any obstacles or difficulties that may arise.

- Critically inspect pre-installed roof access/scaffolding if already supplied. Confirm that its safety compliance ticket has been fully completed. Photograph it. (See details below)

- Only if site conditions are suitable for installation on the day, then fully brief occupants (if any) of work to be carried out, detailing anticipated timescale plus when it will be carried out and where, including access and all health and safety implications of the installation relevant to them.

Scaffolding

It is essential that all work takes place where any fall would be no more than 2m. The implication of this is that the width of any scaffolding normally extends significantly wider than the width of any collector array.

The most secure but time-consuming scaffolds to construct are traditional steel post scaffolds. Specialist portable and lightweight aluminium scaffolds are available on the market.

Portable scaffold
Supplied by Turner Access

Roof access including scaffolding may be sub-contracted to specialists or installers may wish to obtain the relevant qualification themselves.

If installing roof access yourself, carefully erect the roof access equipment according to its instructions, having first provided a firm and level base from which to set this up.

Use undamaged parts and robust timbers and levellers where needed. Include erection of guardrails, toe boards and stabilisers as appropriate.

Where installations exceed one day and where appropriate, remove all access equipment at the end of the day so that it cannot be climbed. Store access equipment in a secure place and re-erect it the next day.

Ensure safe lifting, lowering and storage at height. Safely raise tools, brackets and fixings required for the roof work. Store them in tied-on or otherwise well secured roof buckets, or tool bags or tool belts as appropriate. Do not allow wind to catch large objects such as collectors. Keep them securely attached to flat solid surfaces. Unless the scaffold is specially specified and constructed for overhanging or side-imposed loads, it is advisable to raise all material such as array mounting rails and modules on to the scaffold only from directly underneath, within the secure stable rectangle created by its vertical supports, for example lifted via a slot in its flooring.

Prepare to start the job, if appropriate

Carry out all appropriate on-site health and safety site measures including cordoning off the full working/potential fall area. Unload panels, equipment and tools. Check every single thing that you will need. Preparation now will save time later.

- Assemble and check the conditions and presence of the required tools and parts before you start.

- Make sure that all tools and parts are appropriate and all are available before starting.

- Tick all components off on the relevant parts list one by one and identify each carefully. If items are missing or damaged report this immediately.

- Lay dust sheets on all internal surfaces requiring protection including carpets and vulnerable hard floors.

- Gain access to loft via suitable ladder, temporary ladder or working platforms, and check cable positions, entries and routes against survey data.

- Remove and lay ladders flat in a place where they will not obstruct access if unattended.

- Measure the exact size of your modules/arrays from top to bottom where the supports attach, and record this measurement.

- If necessary, strengthen rafters (or timbers or other structures) used for securing the panel, for example by adding noggins between rafters or adding thicker timbers alongside them.

Working at height

As discussed earlier, most PV arrays are roof mounted or mounted at height. This introduces the increased risk of working at height. Not only should the safety of the installer be considered but also that of the client (and their employees/family) and the general public. An appropriate risk assessment should be carried out prior to any work on a PV system.

The risk of falling or dropping any part of the PV array is affected by the module and framework weight, module area (due to wind) and also the angle of the roof. The risk can be minimised through the use of:

- Scaffolding

- Ladders

- Climbing harness

- 'Cherry picker' elevated platform

Any work, which is more than 2m off the ground, requires the use of lifting/elevating equipment such as ladders and scaffolding and/or climbing harnesses for attaching to the building, especially when working near the building edge.

All scaffolding should be erected and inspected by a competent person prior to use.

- Use of appropriate and safe scaffolding

- Scaffold wheels locked

- Walking boards positioned so not to cause people to trip

- Guard rails and toeboards

- Lifting equipment

Ladders should be tied to prevent slipping sideways or outwards. Ladders should be placed on a horizontal surface and leaning against a vertical surface so that the height of the top of the ladder is four times the distance of the bottom of the ladder from the vertical surface.

Construction information sheet series:

Tower scaffolds	CIS10
General access scaffolds and ladders	CIS49
Personal Protective Equipment (PPE): safety helmets	CIS50

Roof working: general

Required competence MUST include Safe Working at Heights and on roof training. Two people are required.

With the client, reconfirm array location. Decide exactly where on the roof your installation is to go.

If necessary pre-drill the roof fixing whilst on the ground.

Roof coverings

In assessing roof coverings, guidelines should be adopted as to when the roof work is beyond the competence of the installer and is best left to roofing specialists.

Slates needs to be laid in a brick-like bond with a double lap to avoid water entry around the sides, but even with this required double lap, they tend to be lighter per square metre than both plain and interlocking tiles. Slates do not have locating lugs (nibs) on the back (as do both types of tile) and so each slate needs to be individually positioned and nailed into place on the roofing battens, therefore roofing with slates can be more time consuming than either of the tiles. They are usually suitable for pitched roofs with a slope of 23° or greater, larger slates can be used for even lower slopes. Alternatives to natural slate are man-made alternatives (below), some are lighter and most are cheaper.

Interlocking tiles are typically made from concrete with a profile that allows the tiles to overlap each other, side to side, giving much better protection from the ingress of water. Typically sized 380x230mm with an effective width of 200mm (i.e. 30mm overlap). They are normally laid in straight lines up the roof with a single lap. They tend to be heavier per square metre than slate but lighter than plain tiles. Locating lugs (nibs) on the back are used to mount them on the roofing battens. They are usually suitable for pitched roofs with a slope of 23° or greater.

Plain tiles were traditionally made from clay but are now increasingly concrete and are generally sized about 265 x 165mm. They need to be laid in a brick-like bond with a double lap to avoid water entry around the sides. Due to the required double lap, they tend to be heavier per square metre than both slate and interlocking tiles. Locating lugs (nibs) on the back are used to mount them on the roofing battens. These are usually suitable for pitched roofs with a slope of 35° or greater.

As for ease of installation, concrete pantiles are generally single lapped and are often only fastened at the ridges, gables and eaves and around any roof opening. They permit easy installation of roof hooks since they can be pushed up underneath the tile above or with care removed for modification. A series of pushed-up tiles are used as means of moving around the roof by roofers as long as care is taken not to damage the underlying sarking. However, double lapped slates provide a more difficult installation, since they are all fastened in place and form a more fragile roof covering that may break when walked upon, particularly in the case of natural slate that has weathered on an older roof.

Underfelt or sarking is a layer of material between the back of the slate/tiles and the roof frame providing slight insulation and an extra waterproof barrier for any moisture. It is traditionally made from bitumen, with a strong woven base. This base is liable to become brittle with age and rot where exposed to sunlight. Modern alternatives are generally lighter and more durable.

While in England, Wales and Ireland the weatherproof layer of the roof consists of a sarking of felt or membrane over the rafters (trusses), held in place with battens that are used to support the tiles or slates and allow fixings to be fastened, in Scotland, tightly fitting timber sarking is used instead.

Boarded flat roofs are normally covered in a two or three layers system bonded using hot bitumen or a flame torch. Each layer has traditionally been bitumen-based, however high performance polymer based materials are available which offer better performance. Usually for bitumen based materials, all the layers are put down using hot bitumen or a flame torch with the top layer being covered in protective mineral chippings or painted with a solar reflective protective coating.

Any penetration of these layers will need to be resealed to maintain the waterproofing.

If you do not feel confident in tackling this area of work arrange for a roofing professional to carry it out for you.

Roofing structures

The work required on a roof is an important part of a PV installation although electricians are generally unfamiliar with it. There are several aspects of this type of work, which you will have to become familiar with:

- Roofing terminology

- Roofing knowledge; lifting and replacing tiles, reinstating weatherproof seals

Roofing terms

In order to understand and describe how a PV mounting system will work, we must have a basic knowledge and understanding of a roofing structure and the terms used to describe certain parts of that structure.

Pitched roof – This is used to describe a sloped roof. The pitch is also the angle at which the roof sits from the horizontal.

Hip – An external sloping edge, which joins two pitched roof slopes.

Hipped roof – Where all the sections of the roof are sloped. There are no gable ends on a hipped roofed house.

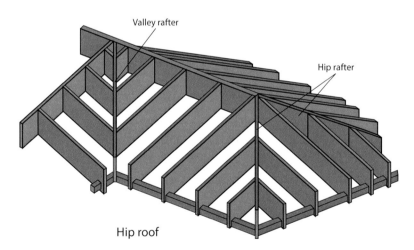

Hip roof

A hipped roof has more slopes than a gable end roof. This means there is a greater chance of the roof having a south-facing slope. However, the slopes at the end of the building (Hip slopes) may also be smaller and will be less likely to be rectangular, making it difficult to fit a PV array.

Gable (end) – The triangular section of the wall at the end of the house, which supports the two sections of sloped roof.

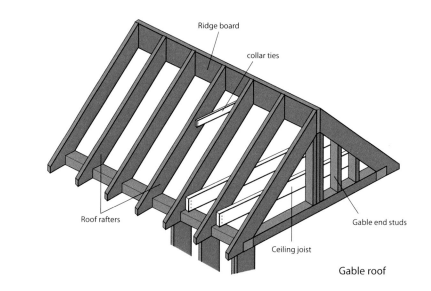

Half hipped roof – A ridge roof finishing at a gable of which a small section of the top is angled or hipped, the rest being vertical.

Rafter – These are sloping roof timbers, which support battens and tiles or slates. These are typically at 450mm centres but can also be at 360mm centres. Rafter spacing may need to be checked to determine the number and position of fixing centres for an array mounting system.

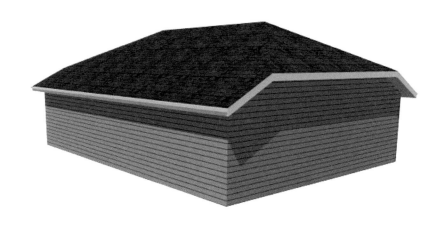

Purlin – The major horizontal roof beam supporting the rafter.

Ridge board – The major horizontal timber along the ridge.

Top plate – The major horizontal timber along the eaves.

Tie-beam – The major horizontal beam across the roof at the eaves.

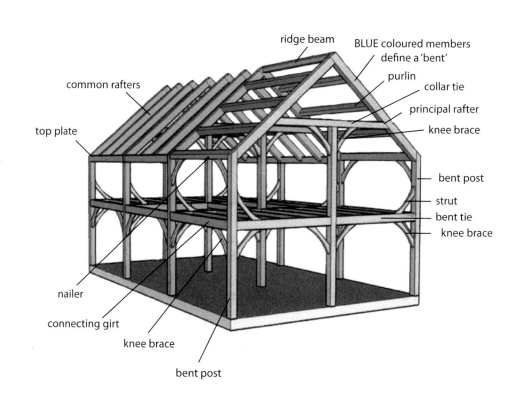

Roofing terms

Strut – Vertical or near vertical support for rafters/purlins.

Battens – Thin timber strips to which the tiles and slates are fixed.

Sarking/Felt – Underfelting used beneath battens/tiles on pitched roofs.

Counterbattening – Thin strips of wood are fixed on top of the sarking/felt vertically and screwed into the rafters. Battens are then fixed on top of the counterbattens horizontally and then the tiles or slates are fixed to the battens. For a roof integrated system, this allows a greater amount of air to circulate between the modules and the sarking/felt. This is advisable for this type of integrated system as it will keep the modules cooler, thus increasing the voltage output and in turn, the power output of the array.

Flashing – A strip of metal to prevent water entering at a joint in the roofing.

(Image courtesy of www.rd.com)

Noggins – Strips of wood, which are screwed to the side of the rafter to allow a fixing.

Roofs are normally classified according to their slope:

Flat Roofs:	Slope less than 5°
Slightly sloped roofs:	Slope 5-22°
Normally sloped roof:	Slope 22-45°
Steep roof:	Slope greater than 45°

Roofing knowledge

Most PV systems that are installed in the UK are on the roofs of buildings. Integrated and non-integrated modules have different requirements when it comes to mounting, ventilation and weather sealing.

Sloped roofs

When dealing with a sloped roof, the roof skin is considerably different to that of a flat roof. On a sloped roof, the skin is regarded as a roof covering, which uses such tiles and slate. These are laid counter to the rainwater flow direction and require a minimum roof slope according to the covering type. Guidance on building structure calculations can be found under the calculation section of this manual.

When dealing with the roofing structure, it is imperative that the weatherproof function of the roof covering has been maintained after the installation of the PV system. Below are some items to look for:

- No roof timbers or felt has been left exposed

- No cracked or missing tiles

- Appropriate flashing at the edge of any roof covering (e.g. at the edge of a roof-integrated PV system or where a tile has been removed for a non-integrated frame fixing point).

All roofs, regardless of whether PV is installed or not, must have ventilated roof spaces to meet the current building regulation standards. This is often achieved via ventilation tiles or roof vents/pipes. It is important that these methods of ventilation are not obstructed or removed when installing a PV system. It may be possible to move the ventilation tiles to another part of the roof. Alternatively, the PV array may be positioned to avoid a ventilation tile or pipe. In some cases, roof vents may be installed at the eaves.

Rafters may also be too thin to accept the holding screws from the mounting system, therefore noggins would have to be fitted to the rafter to allow a secure fixing.

The structural design and integrity of the roof should be assessed before installation work commences.

MCS pitched roof system requirements

PV systems mounted above or integrated into a sloped roof should utilise products that have been tested and approved to MCS012 (test procedures used to demonstrate the performance of solar systems under the action of wind loads, fire, rainfall and wind driven rain).

- **In roof (Integrated) products (e.g. PV tiles)** – all fixing and flashing components used to mount and make weather-tight the solar roofing product must be packaged and listed as part of a complete kit that includes the PV module. The MCS installer must ensure that the system is installed to comply with the manufacturer's instructions.

- **In roof (Integrated) mounting system** – All fixing and flashing components used to mount and make weather-tight the PV system must be specifically approved to work together (e.g. supplied and listed as a kit of parts) and listed to work with either the named PV module, or listed as a universal type where PV module type is immaterial to the performance of the system. The MCS installer must ensure that the system is installed to comply with the manufacturer's instructions for both the mounting system components and the PV module.

- **Above roof (non-Integrated) mounting systems** – All components used to mount the system must be specifically approved to work together or be listed as universal components. The mounting system must also be listed to work with either the named PV module, or listed as a universal type where PV module type is immaterial to the performance of the system. The MCS installer must ensure that the system is installed to comply with the manufacturer's instructions for both the mounting system components and the PV module.

In all cases it is expected that the manufacturers' fixing instructions are followed with respect to wind loading. Wind loads vary from site to site and the installer must ensure that the design wind load is within the range as specified by the manufacturer; and/or for high wind sites, any required additional fixings are correctly installed. Where an installer has chosen to utilise a mounting assembly comprised of "universal" components, the installer must ensure that all components are suitable for the wind load imposed on that component. Guidance on wind loading and fixing calculations can be found under the calculation section of this manual.

Tile types

There are many types of tiles that are used in the UK but before we have look at some, we should cover some tile terminology.

Lap – This is the overlap between the tiles.

Course – This is each horizontal line of tiles.

Tile head – This is the top of the tile.

Tile tail – This is the bottom of the tile.

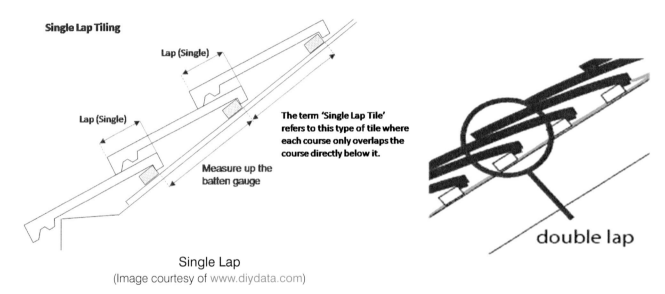

Single Lap
(Image courtesy of www.diydata.com)

When looking at different tile types, it is important to understand the description and how these tiles are installed.

Pantiles – Also known as single lap profiled tiles, these tiles have an s-shaped section. These tiles interlock with one another, using a hook like system. The left hand edge of one tile has grooves on it which face upwards. The tile to the left of this one has hooks on the right hand side of it which face downwards. These two edges interlock and this is the same for all tiles on that course. This type of tile is simply hung on the battens by means of a small 'nib' on the back of the head of the tile, thus making them easy to slide into place. These tiles should be nailed every few courses.

Flat tile – Ordinary flat roofing tiles usually have dimensions of 265 x 165mm and are often referred to as 'plain tiles'. This type of tile is usually 'double lapped' where there is normally two thickness of tile over the roof and one tile overlaps the other. These tiles also have 'nibs' on the back of the head of the tile. Again, these tiles should also be nailed every few courses.

Slate – Slate roofs are significantly different to tiled roofs. Slates have no 'nibs' on the back of them and so cannot sit on the batten, therefore, each individual slate has to be nailed down using two nails. The edges of the slates are normally aligned with the middle of the slates above and below them. With both slates and plain tiles, they employ the 'double head lap' system where the head of each slate or tile is covered by two slates or tiles.

Flat roofs

The roof covering concerning flat roofs is roof sealing. This is a fully waterproof layer over the entire surface of the roof and can be made of bitumen roofing felt, plastic roof sheeting or plastics that are applied as a fluid and then harden. These types of sealants are absolutely essential for roofs with less than a 5° slope.

The structural design and integrity of the roof should be assessed before installation work commences.

Module fixing

PV modules/arrays can be mounted almost anywhere on the externals of a building. The following points on the building structure are areas to consider when looking for array positions:

- Sloped Roofs (Non-integrated and Integrated systems)

- Flat Roofs (Non-integrated and Integrated systems)

- Façades (Non-integrated and Integrated systems)

The manufacturer's instructions should always be observed when designing a PV array mounting structure. In particular, attention shall be paid to the clamping zones as prescribed by each manufacturer as these will often vary.

To ensure PV mounting systems meet the required specification for wind loads, fire, rainfall and wind driven rain, installers and designers should use products which are certified under MCS standards MCS012 (Pitched Roof Installation Kits) and MCS017 (Bespoke Building Integrated Photovoltaic Products). These standards become compulsory in September 2013 and May 2013 respectively. This is recommended even if MCS compliance is not required.

This information is from the MCS guide to installation of PV systems.

Each has its own unique fixing systems and should be considered separately when deciding on which fixing system suits the intended purpose.

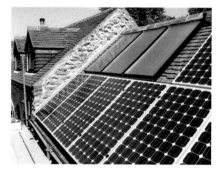
Sloped Roof System
(Image courtesy of
www.daviddarling.info)

Flat Roof System
(Image courtesy of
www.coolflatroof.com)

Facade Mounted System
(Image courtesy of
www.suntech-power.com)

Sloped roofs

When considering PV arrays to be mounted on sloped roofs, these fall into two different categories:

- Non-integrated modules/arrays (on-roof systems)

- Integrated modules/arrays (in-roof systems)

We shall consider these systems separately as they have different installation methods.

Non-integrated systems

Using this system, the array is fitted above the existing roof covering using a metal frame or substructure, leaving the roof covering intact and continuing to provide its waterproofing function. This method is the most commonly used type when fixing an array to an existing sloped roof, as this is the most cost-efficient option.

The frame or substructure contains three components:

- Roofing mounts

- Mounting rails

- Module fixings

The roof mounts are attached to the roof structure beneath the roof covering (tiles, slates etc) and the rail system is then anchored to the roof mounts. The modules are then attached to the rail system using system-specific fixings. Secure fixing points have to be established to enable the substructure to be constructed. This substructure will support the PV modules and the roof has to be resealed around these fixing points.

The array fixing brackets should not affect the weather proofing of the roof they are fitted to. For example, systems attached to tile roofs should be designed and installed such that the fixing brackets do not displace the tiles and cause gaps more than naturally occurs between the tiles. Fixing methods must not subject roof coverings to imposed loads which may degrade their primary purpose of maintaining weather proofing.

The roof sarking/felt should be inspected for damage during installation works. Any damage should be repaired or the sarking/felt replaced as necessary. Damaged sarking/felt will not provide an effective weather and air barrier and can affect weather tightness and the wind loads imposed on the roof cladding.

This substructure must be able to withstand the forces that it will encounter during its operating lifetime and transfer these forces to the roofing structure without, at the same time supporting itself on the roof covering.

The modules are then attached to the rail system using system-specific fixings.

Sloped roofs

Non-integrated systems

There are certain push and pull factors exerted on these modules when they are installed using a non-integrated method. These push factors are a result of snow load, impact pressure from wind and also the individual weight of the modules and the substructure itself. The pull factors are mainly from the pulling effect of winds, which can draught under the modules and act like the sail of a boat. In order to minimize these forces, the following should be considered:

- The gap between the module surface and the roof covering should be kept to a minimum without affecting the effective ventilation of the array.

- Modules should not extend beyond the vertical and horizontal lines of the building (roof ridge, eaves, gable etc). Information given from the MCS guide to installation of PV systems states "unless specifically designed to do so, systems should be kept away from the roof perimeter. For a domestic roof, a suitable minimum clearance zone is around 400-500mm".

  The requirement to keep an array away from the edge of a roof is suggested due to:

  - Wind loads are higher at edge zones.

  - Keeping edge zones clear facilitates better access for maintenance and fire services.

- Taking arrays close to the roof edge may adversely affect rain drainage routes.

- When retro fitting systems, there is a potential for damage to ridge, hip, valley or eaves details.

On many roofs, a 500mm gap from the edge of the roof will still constitute that PV modules are fitted in the "edge zone" as defined by BS EN 1991-1 where higher pressure coefficients need to be implemented due to higher imposed wind loads. This information has been taken from the MCS guidance document.

- Module surfaces should have the same angle of slope as the roof.

- Modules should have a small gap between them (approximately 10mm) to reduce pressure built up behind the array. This will also reduce whistling sounds during windy conditions.

Structural specifications are usually given in tabulated format from the assembly and module manufacturer, where it is possible to calculate minimum number of roof fixings per m2 and maximum span between supports.

Roof mounts

The choice of roof mounts mainly depends on the type of existing roof covering. There are rafter-dependant and rafter-independent solutions. Whilst rafter-independent fixings, which are attached to the roof battens, offer greater flexibility for positioning, they do not have the same capability as rafter-dependant fixings to withstand greater loads. We will be looking at rafter-dependant fixings.

Sloped roofs

Non-integrated systems

Rafter-dependant fixings usually come in the shape of roof hooks and come in a range of different sizes and shapes depending upon the existing roof covering.

These are fitted directly to the rafter through the sarking/felt using an appropriate fixing screw/bolt.

Tiles or slates removed for fixing a mounting bracket should be re-attached to include a means of mechanical fixing.

Roof Hooks
(Image courtesy of www.evoenergy.co.uk)

Historically, some mounting systems on slate or tile roofs have relied on a simple "through bolt" approach. However, this fixing method has the potential for the fixing bolts or sealing washer cracking the slates/tiles beneath them. It can also present difficulties with ensuring the long term weather tightness and durability of the roof penetration.

Through bolts shall only be used on tile or slate roofs where the following requirements are met:

1. The bolt or flashing shall not transfer any load on the slates/tiles beneath.

2. The system shall not rely on silicone or other mastic sealant to provide a weather-tight seal.

3. The system must durably seal every layer of roof covering that is perforated by the bolt system.

4. The system shall not rely on a sealing washer or plate that presses down on the slate/tile to ensure a weather-tight seal.

5. The bolt fixings shall not be into battens.

Information on through bolt systems is guidance from the MCS guide to installation of PV systems.

Sloped roofs

Non-integrated systems

Rail systems

Rails, which are mounted on the roof mounts, support the PV modules. The common used arrangement is for the rails to be mounted horizontally (two used for each row), across the roof surface and the PV modules laid vertically (portrait). The distance between the rails depends upon the available fixing points for the roof mounts. If required, the rails can be mounted vertically with the modules being mounted horizontally (landscape).

Thermal expansion should be considered when installing larger arrays. The module and mounting system manufacturer should be consulted to determine the maximum array width and continuous rail length that can be permitted without the need for an expansion gap.

Portrait Orientation
(Image from "A Top to Bottom Perspective on a PV system" by John Wiles, Nov-Dec, 2008. Used by permission of IAEI News.)

Landscape Orientation
(Image courtesy of www.wattsun.com)

Clamp fixings are normally adopted for a rail system. A double-sided centre clamp is usually used between two modules and a single-sided clamp is used at the end of each row. These are held in place using assembly screws that slot into grooves on the rails. The screw length or clamp height, are selected in accordance with the module frame depth.

The actual mounting of on-roof systems is broadly similar regardless of manufacturer but there are differences so careful attention must be paid to the specific instructions for the system you are fitting.

The components shown here are fairly common with the main difference being the use of bolts or Allen screws.

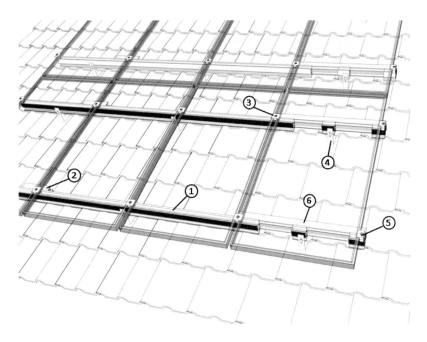

On roof rail system

1 – Base rail   2 – Joiner piece   3 – Inter-module clamp

4 – Roof hook   5 – Module end-clamp   6 – Telescoping end piece (optional)

The following is an example of the instructions from one manufacturer.

First define the size of the array/module field.

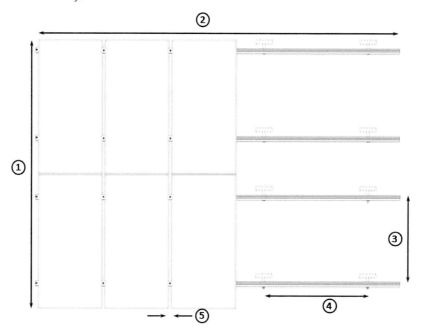

The distances between roof connections for a portrait installation are specified. Clamp-on roof hooks, roof hooks and hanger bolts need to be installed in specific distances, depending on the distance of rafters and the structural conditions of the existing roof.

Height of the module field: module height x number of modules vertically:

1. Width of the module field: number of modules horizontally x (width of the module + 18mm) + 32mm

2. Distance between roof connections vertically (according to the clamping points pre-defined by the module producer): Quarter-points of the modules, about ½ of module height

3. Distance between roof connections horizontally: Depending on the distance between rafters and on the static requirements

4. Distance between modules: 17mm

When positioning the modules, please take into consideration:

That dimensions of tiles or other roof covering and the position of the rafters define the precise actual horizontal distance between roof connections.

That the distance between roof laths defines the precise actual vertical distance between roof connections.

● Mark the positions of the roof hooks on the tiles.

● Remove the roof tiles at the marked positions or, if possible, simply push them up.

- Position the roof hooks above the low parts of the tiles.

- Fix the roof hooks to the rafter using three 6 x 80mm wood screws.

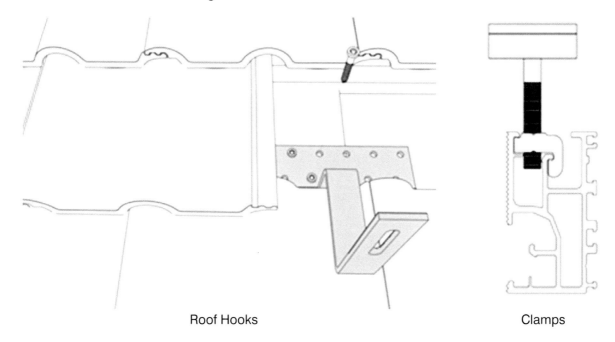

Roof Hooks   Clamps

- Fit the rails to the roof hooks using the clamps.

- Only tighten the bolts when the rails are fully aligned.

- Use joiner pieces where necessary for long runs.

- **DO NOT** use the rails as a ladder, they will not take the point load and may damage the tiles underneath.

- The modules are successively mounted onto the base rails.

- It is recommended to start on one side of the module field.

- When using telescoping end-pieces, start installing the modules on the rail side of each row, so that the telescoping end-piece can be aligned with the last module to be mounted.

- Add anti-slip protection, consisting of a bolt and nut inserted into the holes on the underside of the module frame, to the lowest row of modules (horizontal rail installation only). This keeps the modules from sliding off and thus facilitates installation.

- The anti-slip protection does not have any static function in the finished installation.

- The modules are fixed with inter-module clamps and end-clamps. An end-clamp will hold one module, an inter-module clamp two consecutive ones.

Anti-slip installation

- The anti-slip protection is only necessary on the lowermost row of modules.

- Fit two bolts M6 x 20 and nuts into the lower holes of each module.

- Place the first module of the bottom row so that the anti-slip protection sits in the rail channel of the lowest row of rails.

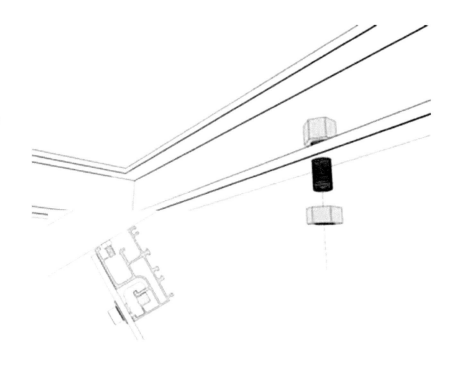

End-clamp installation

- Slide the clamp into the rail channel.

- Align the module and push the module end-clamp firmly against the side of the module.

- Tighten the Allen bolt and clamp (tightening torque 8Nm).

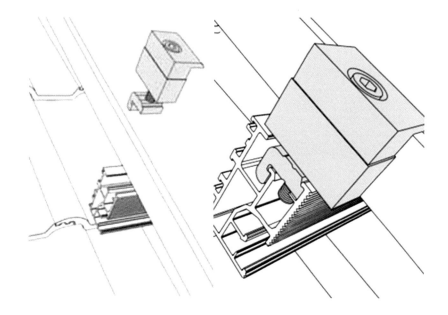

Inter-module clamp installation

- Slide the clamp into the rail channel.

- Push the inter-module clamp firmly against the already fixed module.

- Push the next module against the other side of the module end-clamp.

- Tighten the allen bolt and clamp (tightening torque 8Nm).

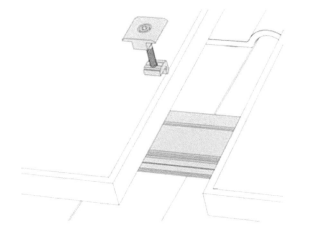

Installation of further rows

- Set the modules of the next row above the lowest row of modules. For optical reasons, a gap can be left between module rows.

- Use a spare inter-module clamp as a gauge for the space between module rows. In this way, the horizontal and vertical gaps between modules will be identical.

- Fix the modules to the base rails using inter-module clamps and module end-clamps, as described above for the first row of modules.

- Connect the modules in series into arrays to match the design specification of the installation.

Sloped roofs

Integrated systems

Integrated systems can be the same modules used for non-integrated systems or purpose built PV 'tiles', which would replace the normal roof tiles.

For integrated systems, the PV modules replace the existing roof covering. Either the entire or partial roof area is covered using the modules. Due to this system replacing the existing roof covering, the installer has to ensure that the same level of rainproofing is guaranteed when the array is completed. The angle of slope also has to be carefully scrutinised, if the slope of the array is less

Integrated Roof tiles
(Image courtesy of www.treehugger.com)

than that of the roof, it would be deemed that the structure is no longer considered to be sufficiently rainproof. Sufficient ventilation behind the array must also be looked at in order to avoid moisture on the back of the modules.

With integrated or in-roof systems the tiles or slates are removed from the area of roof to be covered by the PV modules and a waterproof membrane is then secured over the underlying roof structure and under the roof tiles surrounding the exposed area. The bottom edge of the membrane is lapped over the bottom row of tiles so that water is forced back up onto the roof. The mounting rails are then fixed through the membrane into the roof timbers in a similar manner to those used for on roof systems.

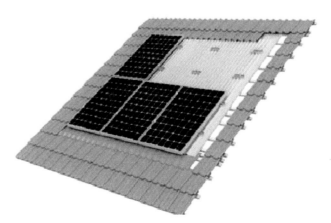

In-roof mounting arrangements

Soakaways are fixed around the sides of the exposed area and the modules are then mounted on the fixings brackets/rails. When the modules are fixed in place, seals/adaptors are used between the panels to discourage water penetration although any water passing between the modules will be diverted down under the modules and back out onto the roof by the membrane. Finally a top flashing is fitted under the top row of tiles and over the top edge of the modules to ensure water flows over the modules rather than under.

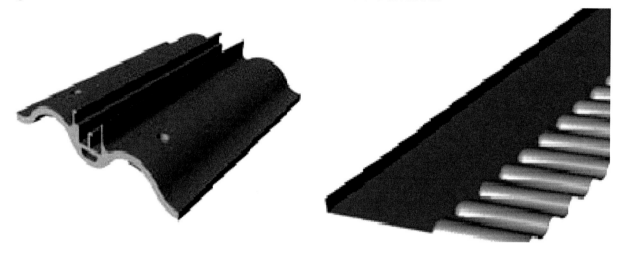

Waterproof adaptor and top flashing

The actual installation process and materials used varies between manufacturers such as GSE plastic panels or with viridian panel frames with most systems requiring specialist training from the manufacture, the following is an example from one.

As with on-roof mounted systems the first thing to do is calculate the size of the module/array field.

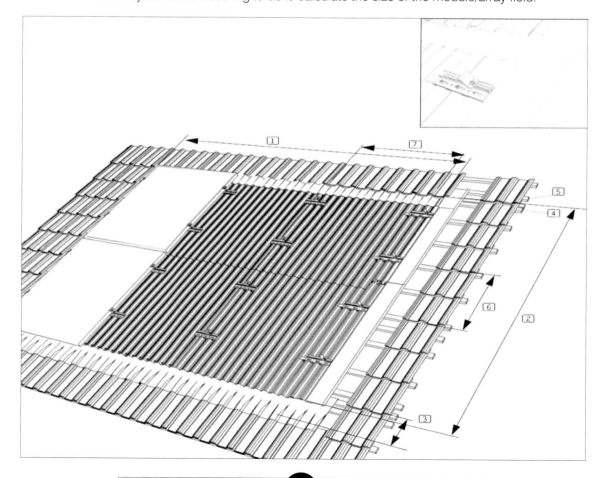

1. Width of the module field:
   Module width x number of modules horizontally + ((number of modules horizontally – 1) x 19mm) + 50mm.

2. Height of the module field: Module length x number of modules vertically + ((number of modules vertically – 1) x 19mm).

3. Additional roof battens for fixing the sealing strip: Distance between new batten (centre) and edge of the below tiles: 120mm or 220mm, depending on the chosen sealing strip.

4. Additional roof battens for fixing the upper edge of the PV field: Height of the module field – 30mm (centre of batten).

5. Additional roof battens for fixing the top flashing: Height of the module field + 280mm (centre of batten).

6. Vertical distance between adapters: Approximately at quarter points of the module = ½ module length (observe the information provided by the module manufacturer). Spacing is based on the roof batten raster. In the case of a particularly unfortunate batten raster, additional battens may have to be installed).

7. Horizontal distance between adapters: Can be calculated from the module dimensions. Position the adapter in the inner part of the module field so that its centre point is located in the 19mm clearance space between the modules. A minimum distance of 25mm must separate the adapter edge of the adapters on the right and left edge and the module field edge.

Remove roof covering for the surface area of the modules. On the lateral and top edges remove an additional row of tiles beyond what is necessary for the actual module field.

In the case of an uneven roof truss, it may be necessary to adjust the height of the roof battens.

If necessary, lay a roofing membrane under the intended module field. Should the insulation be in direct contact with the roofing membrane, the vapour permeability of the roofing membrane must be ensured.

Unroll the sealing strip along the lower edge of the uncovered roof surface.

Cut the sealing strip for the length of the surface area + one extra tile width on the left and right.

Allow for adequate spacing (5 cm) between the upper edge of the roof tile and the lower edge of the corrugated metal sheet to avoid an edge that is too sharp. Also allow for adequate overlapping by the corrugated sheets.

After fixing the sealing strip, adapt the shape of the strip to the shape of the tiles, taking care to avoid the formation of sharp edges.

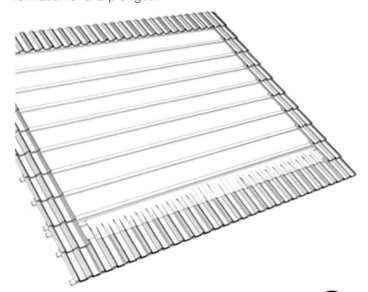

Note: The sealing strip must vertically overlap the tiles at least as much as the tiles overlap themselves. In case of very curved roof tiles, it may be advisable to flatten the upper edge of the tile underneath the sealing strip prior to laying. In that way, sharp edges and water accumulation can be avoided.

Guide the foam profile filler up to the lateral flashings of the module field.

Fix the profile filler on the sealing strip with double-sided adhesive tape in such a way that later (by means of adapters or calottes), it can be screwed onto the roof batten directly underneath it.

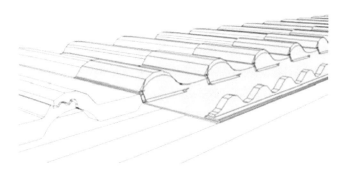

Should Metal Roll be used as the sealing strip, the top 2cm of the adhesive surface can be completely turned over, so that the adhesive surface is facing upwards, and the profile filler can be attached without additional adhesive tape.

Laying the corrugated metal sheets

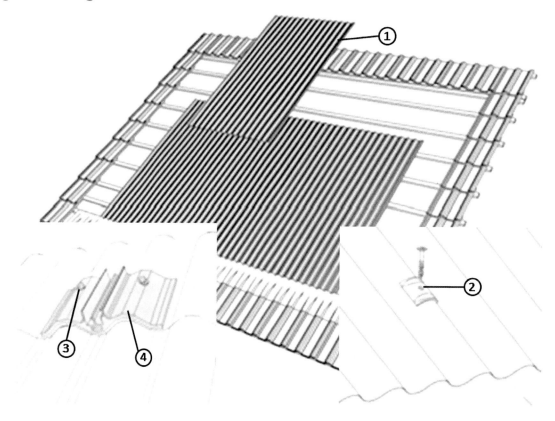

1. Corrugated metal sheet

2. Roofing screw 4.5 x 45mm with calotte

3. Sheet metal screw 6.5 x 65mm (self drilling)

4. Adapter (in this case: short adapter for landscape installation)

If the corrugated metal sheets do not sufficiently overlap, the roof may become subject to leaks.

Sheets must overlap above each other by at least 200mm vertically and by at least 80mm = 2 high points of the corrugation horizontally.

Lay the corrugated sheets in sequence starting from the bottom and working upwards, and plan the side overlap in accordance with the main wind direction.

For normal rectangular roofs, lay the lower edge of the bottom row of corrugated metal sheets parallel to the eaves.

Attach the corrugated metal sheets to the roof with 6.5 x 65mm sheet metal screws together with the adapters, the profile filler and the lateral flashings. If necessary, use additional 4.5 x 45mm roofing screws and calottes, so that at least six fixing points per m² are provided.

Position the corrugated sheets so that they correspond to the entire module field. If necessary, use additional roofing screws and calottes to attach the overlapping points.

After laying the lateral and top flashings, attach the outer edges of the corrugated sheet surface area every 50cm with roofing screws and calottes.

Installing the adaptors (portrait installation)

Walking on the corrugated sheets can cause dents or tears.

Do not walk or stand on the corrugated sheets.

We recommend the use of a roofer's ladder.

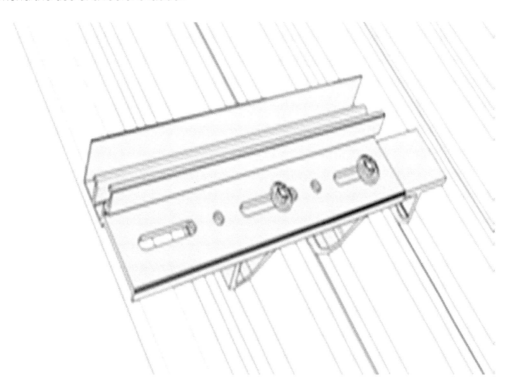

For orientation: Mark the position of the roof battens on the corrugated metal sheet by using a chalk line.

Screw the portrait adapters at the points specified in the planning with two 6.5 x 65mm sheet metal screws each onto the roof batten lying directly underneath. Use the corresponding drill holes in the adapter.

Install the two parts of the portrait adapters in the module field precisely aligned above each other.

For mounting on the lateral edges, the perforated rail can be slid sideways up to 50mm beyond the basis to ensure a clean transition between roof and module field.

Installing the lateral flashings

- Position the lateral flashings so that two waves of the flashing overlap the corrugated metal sheet on the right and left side of the module field.

- Align the sheets on the lower edge of the corrugated metal sheet area.

- If using several lateral flashings, overlap them by at least 200mm vertically – if necessary, shorten the topmost lateral flashing corresponding to the size of the corrugated metal sheet area.

Installing the top flashings

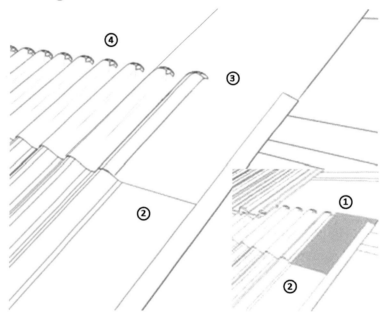

1. Top flashing, a strip of 150mm flattened on the edges (area marked in grey)

2. Lateral flashing

3. Corner flashing

4. Top flashing

Install additional roof battens 30mm below and 280mm above the upper end of the corrugated metal sheet area (measured from the centre of the battens).

Position the left-hand and right-hand corner flashings with the respective two outer corrugations and the flat part overlapping the lateral flashings, and push them downwards as far as they will go. (Alternatively, by use of a rubber hammer, about 150mm of the top flashing can be flattened on the left-hand and right-hand top flashings respectively (see area marked in grey above). The flattened sheets can then be used in place of the corner flashings).

Continue positioning the top flashings, taking care to align them properly and to have them overlap each other by at least 80mm (= two high points of the corrugation). Fix each overlap with an adapter and two screws 6.5 x 65mm (if in the right position) or with a calotte and screw 4.5 x 45mm.

Work the upstand of the flashings with tinsmith tools to ensure a clean overlap.

Fix the upstand to the underlying batten at least every 500mm, using fixing clips and screws 4.5 x 45mm.

Complete the fixation of the top flashings by fixing the corrugated part at least every 500mm, using adapters and/ or calottes and the according screws.

Note: Avoid overtightening the screws as this may distort the flashings and cause water leaks.

Installing the modules (portrait or landscape)

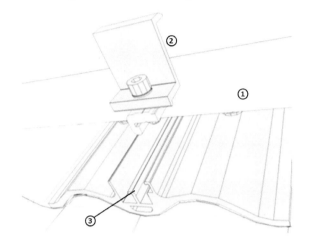

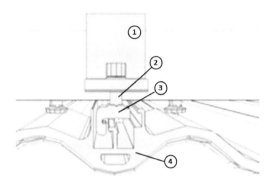

1. PV module
2. Module end-clamp
3. Clamp channel of the adapter

1. Module end-clamp
2. Allen bolt
3. Clamp
4. Adapter

Place the clamp in the track channel of the adapter.

When positioning, the bolt at the bottom side of the clamp may not protrude. The form of the clamp fits precisely into the channel.

Place the module on top and align it.

Slide the end-clamp completely onto the module and tighten it (tightening torque 8Nm), so that there is a minimum of 25mm between the inner side of the end-clamp (on the module frame) and the outer adapter edge.

Attention:

The track channel of the adapter in which the end-clamp is slid, is identical for both, portrait and landscape installation. It is merely turned by 90° and positioned transversely to the overlying module frame.

In order to ensure secure positioning, the clamp must sit completely inside the adapter (at least 5mm distance from the adapter edge).

Attaching the PV modules within the module field (portrait and landscape installation)

Place the clamp in the channel of the adapter.

When positioning, the bolt at the bottom side of the clamp may not protrude. The form of the clamp fits precisely into the channel.

Align the module clamp on the first module and then slide the next module up against the module clamp.

Tighten the module clamp (tightening torque 8Nm), so that both modules are securely fixed.

Continue until all modules are in place.

Retiling the roof

Replace the tiles around the module field.

Depending on the module field and the type of tiles it may be necessary to cut the tiles that abut the field.

Depending on the type of tiles it may be impossible to avoid a gap between the tile and the top or lateral flashings. If this is the case then the gap **MUST** be sealed against snow accumulation and insect or bird penetration.

Flat roofs

When considering PV arrays to be mounted on flat roofs, these fall into two different categories:

- Non-Integrated modules/arrays (on-roof systems)

- Integrated modules/arrays (in-roof systems)

We shall consider these systems separately as they have different installation methods.

Non-integrated systems

These systems work on the same principle as the sloped roof systems, the modules are mounted on a metal frame above the existing roof skin. These arrays are generally fitted to have a favourable angle using the support frame to achieve this.

Mounting the frame to the flat roof is considerably important. This can be achieved in one of two ways: either by a ballast-mounted system or an anchored system. This is usually subject to the structure of the roof. The use of either system is subject to calculation of load as discussed in the sloped roof section.

Any flat roof or ground frame mounted system is going to be subjected to greater wind stresses than any integrated or slope roof mounted system because the wind can get behind the mounting frames and cause greater pressures.

It may be worth considering whether larger gaps are required between modules to allow the wind to pass between them and therefore lessen the 'sail effect' created by a wall of PV modules. Individual manufacturers will be able to provide more guidance on this.

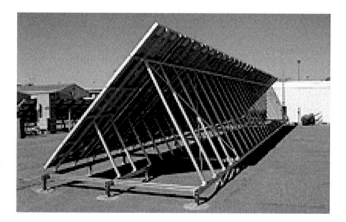

Pole or ground frame mounted systems can be concreted or bolted down securely and the only other matter for consideration is the BS 7671 requirements for steel wire armoured cable and lightning protection (see later in this module).

Where a roof mounted frame is to be used and the roof is of a substantial material such as concrete it is reasonable to assume that the frame can be bolted down securely and that the frame and array will not move. Providing that the weatherproofing can be maintained then no other securing methods will be required. Where the roof is of lighter construction or it is not possible to penetrate the roof material other methods will need to be considered and these are discussed below.

In all cases the cable entry to the building will need to be weatherproof and meet the requirements of BS 7671. The weatherproofing will depend on whether the cable entry is through a flat roof, pitched roof or wall.

There are a number of proprietary flashings and seals available and you should select one according to circumstances. Simply 'tucking' cables though gaps between tiles or drilling holes in tiles and sealing with mastic is not acceptable.

Weatherproof Cable entry
enclosure on flat roof
(Is not good practice)

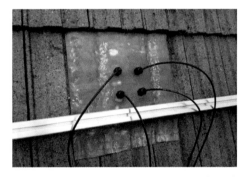

'Home made' flashing on a pitched roof

Wall mounted cable entry

Dektite flashing for pitched roof tile

Ballast-mounted system

Ballast-mounted systems are anchored to the roof without penetrating the roof skin. Concrete slabs, blocks or plinths are placed on the flat roof without further fixing and the support frames are secured to these with screw anchors. Matting should be laid to protect the roof skin from sharp edges of the concrete. This type of system should only be used if the roof can support the calculated load of the array.

There are various types of ballasted mounting systems available from alloy frames to 'plastic' boxes. The method of anchoring is to ballast the frame with heavy weights such as concrete blocks, sacks of sand etc.

| Ballasted mounting box | Ballasted alloy frame |

In most cases the rear legs of the frame will be adjustable to facilitate angling the array for optimum irradiance.

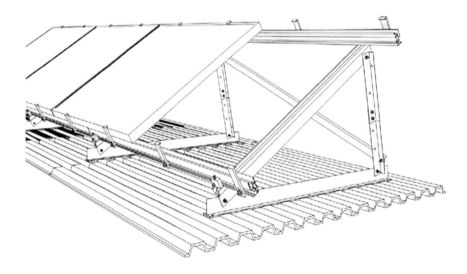

In areas where strong winds are a regular feature it is worth considering additional anchors and guy wires to further secure an angled mounting frame from a 'sail effect' problem

Anchoring system

The supporting frames for the array are mounted on cross beams that are secured either to the roof structure itself or to the roof parapet. If the roof skin is penetrated, the anchorage points must be carefully sealed to the same degree as was there before penetration. When designing the layout, the number of anchorage points that penetrate the roof skin should be kept to a minimum.

Flat roofs

Integrated systems

Integrated systems on flat roofs are uncommon due to the lack of module tilt angle and increased module temperature. This results in lower solar irradiance and thus lower power outputs. This system also suffers from a lack of cleaning by the rain, which increases the need for more frequent maintenance of the modules.

Façade systems

When considering PV arrays to be mounted on façades, these fall into two different categories:

- Non-Integrated Modules/Arrays

- Integrated Modules/Arrays

Non-integrated systems

These can be easily fixed to buildings as would a sign or any other covering. As the modules are not required to provide weatherproofing, they are not held to any particular pattern or layout and can be used to help the aesthetics of the building. They are however, subject to the relevant building regulations and codes of practice.

Integrated systems

Modules that are to be used in an integrated system are required to act either as the external cladding or even the complete external skin of a building. These are referred to as cold and warm façades respectively. Cold façades have no load-bearing element and have an air gap between them and the exterior wall behind them to allow water and moisture to disperse. Warm façades provide some structural support and also weather protection and thermal insulation. This means that these modules are not ventilated and so they must have a lower voltage value (normally using opaque glass to reduce the irradiance level). The fixing systems for these can be complex and the manufacturer or a qualified glazer should be contacted.

Increased roof loading

Section 4 of Approved Document A of the Building Regulations requires that where work involves 'a significant change in the load' on the roof being worked on then the roof structure should be checked to ensure that it is no less compliant with the building regulations than before work commenced.

This means that any dead load or wind lift will be sustained and transmitted via the roof and walls to the ground. This is why it is critical to anchor the mounting system to the structural timbers, i.e. the trusses, rafters etc. and not the lathes or battens.

A significant change in roof load is when loading is increased by more than 15%.

Where it is suspected that the additional loading cannot be sustained then additional work will be required to ensure that the load can be supported before commencing the installation of the PV system.

Ventilation of modules

Sufficient ventilation must be provided behind an array for cooling (typically a minimum 25mm vented air gap to the rear). For building integrated systems, this is usually addressed by the provision of a vented air space behind the modules. On a conventional pitched roof, batten cavity ventilation is typically achieved by the use of counterbattens over the roof membrane and by the installation of eaves and ridge ventilation.

Solar tracker

Solar trackers are used to track the path of the sun either daily or annually. By doing this, the energy gains, compared with a horizontal surface, are 50% in the summer and 30% in the winter.

Solar trackers are normally free standing and would be mounted in a garden or on a flat roof to allow the array to move and the optimum tilt angle and position to be achieved. This can be done either manually or automatically using an electric motor.

Solar trackers that follow the sun's path annually are relatively easy to implement as the array only needs to be adjusted at large intervals (normally weeks or months). These are not normally automatic and would be adjusted manually.

Solar trackers that follow the sun's daily path are much more complicated. This would normally be done using an automatic system where a sensor controlled tracking system would be in place. Light sensors are used to point the modules/array to the brightest point in the sky. Daily solar tracking can also be achieved using an astronomical method where an electronic control system calculates the current position of the sun at the location of the array and a tracking motor moves the modules perpendicular to the sun at preset time intervals.

Solar trackers are also designed to work on either a single axis or dual axis tracking system. The single axis system operates by adjusting the vertical tilt angle of the array but the horizontal angle is usually fixed. A dual axis system can have both vertical and horizontal tilt angle adjustment.

Risk assessment

Risk assessment is a very important step to be considered before the installation of a PV system. A risk assessment is simply a careful examination of what, in your work, could cause harm to people, these are then weighed up to decide whether enough precautions have been taken or more should be done to prevent harm. Workers and others have a right to be protected from harm caused by a failure to take reasonable control measures. The following has been identified by the HSE as the correct method for carrying out a risk assessment:

How to assess the risks at your workplace

Follow these five steps:

1. Identify the hazards

2. Decide who might be harmed and how

3. Evaluate the risks and decide on the precaution

4. Record your findings and implement them

5. Review your assessment and update if necessary

When thinking about your risk assessment, remember:

- A **hazard** is anything that may cause harm, such as chemicals, electricity, working from ladders, an open drawer, etc; and

- The **risk** is the chance, high or low, that somebody could be harmed by these and other hazards, together with an indication of how serious the harm could be.

For more information, visit the HSE website – http://www.hse.gov.uk/risk/assessment.htm where you can download a risk assessment form and policy template. The website also has risk assessment examples, case studies and risk assessment guidance.

All tools, materials and equipment required for the installation should be inspected and ensured that they are in a safe and usable condition before the installation begins.

The handling, moving and storing of PV modules and any equipment associated with the installation should comply with the manufacturer's instructions and also the Manual Handling Operations Regulations 1992 (as amended in 2002).

It is important to note that PV modules are live from point of manufacture and therefore care must be taken when storing and handling modules. Storing modules should be in accordance with manufacturer's instructions.

Although the modules are supplied with pre-made DC tails with proprietary cable connectors that offer finger protection, it is important to remember that the modules are electrically live from the point of manufacture and therefore care must be taken when handling and storing module.

Sequence of works

All DC wiring should if possible be completed prior to installing a solar PV array. This will allow effective electrical isolation of the DC system (via the DC switch-disconnector and PV module cable connectors) while the array is installed; and effective electrical isolation of the PV array while the inverter is installed. Typically this would require an installation of:

- DC switch-disconnector and DC junction box(es)

- String/array positive and negative cables – from the DC switch-disconnector/junction box to either end of the PV string/array;

- PV array main cables from DC switch-disconnector to the inverter.

This should be carried out in such a way that it should never be necessary for an installer to work in any enclosure or situation featuring simultaneously accessible live PV string positive and negative parts. While the installer will be handling live cables during the subsequent module installation, because the circuit is broken at the DC switch-disconnector, there is no possibility of an electric shock current flowing from the partially completed PV string. The maximum electric shock voltage that should ever be encountered is that of one individual PV module. Where it is not possible to pre-install a DC switch-disconnector (for example, a new-build project where a PV array is installed prior to the plant room being completed), cable ends/connectors should be placed temporarily into an isolation box and suitably labelled. Cables are to be well supported, especially those cables exposed to the wind. Cables must be routed in prescribed zones or within mechanical protection, fully supported/cable tied (using UV stabilised ties) and they must also be protected from sharp objects.

Live working

Due to the nature of PV installation work, live working is almost unavoidable. However, given the nature of the system design and so long as the system is designed to fully meet the requirements set out for shock protection by the use of double or reinforced insulation, working on one conductor only represents a small risk which is usually mitigated by the use of appropriate tooling and operative care.

If it is unavoidable to work in any enclosure containing both positive and negative connections that are simultaneously live, work must be performed either by utilising insulating gloves and tools, insulating materials for shrouding purposes and appropriate PPE.

These situations are only likely to arise whilst working on larger systems and wherever possible, these situations should be avoided by following the advice given in the Sequence of Works section.

A temporary warning sign and barrier must be posted/displayed for any period while live PV array cables or other DC cables are being installed.

Shock hazard

It is important to note that, despite all the above precautions, an installer or maintenance engineer may still encounter an electric shock hazard, therefore:

Always test for the presence of voltage of parts before touching any part of the system.

An electric shock may be experienced from a capacitive discharge – a charge may build up in the PV system due to its distributed capacitance to earth. Such effects are more prevalent in certain types of modules and systems, namely amorphous silicon (thin film) modules with metal frames or steel backing. In such circumstances, appropriate and safe live working practices must be adopted.

An example of where such hazards may be encountered is the case where an installer is seated on an earthed metal roof whilst wiring a large PV array. In such circumstances the installer could touch the PV cabling and might get an electric shock to earth. The electric shock voltage will increase with the number of series connected modules. The use of insulating tools and gloves, together with insulating matting to stand or sit on, could mitigate this hazard.

An electric shock may also be experienced due to the PV array developing an earth leakage path. Good wiring practice, double insulation and modules of double or reinforced insulation (Class II) construction can significantly reduce this problem but in any installed systems, leakage paths may still occur. Any person working on a PV system must be aware of this and take the necessary precautions.

Protection for safety – earthing and bonding, RCD and surge protection

Earthing and bonding

Earthing

The earthing and bonding of the AC side of the installation should be installed in accordance with BS7671. The method of protection against electric shock would normally be afforded by ADS for fault protection and barriers & enclosures and insulation for basic protection. Automatic Disconnection of the Supply (ADS) is affected by protective devices that automatically disconnect the supply such as circuit breakers, RCD's, fuses and RCBO's and effective earthing and bonding.

The DC part of the installation is quite different. For the majority of installations, the method of protection against electric shock, both basic and fault protection, will be double or reinforced insulation if the modules are Class II equipment. This means that ADS, as a protective measure, would not be used as there is no earth potential present to safely operate a protective device.

Bonding

Bonding is a measure that is applied to parts that may give rise, under fault conditions to a potential different from that of earth. The measure involves connecting these parts together to reduce any difference in potential if a fault occurs.

When designing the earthing and bonding arrangements of a PV array frame, it is important to understand the various terms, in order to ensure the correct measures are installed.

a) **Protective equipotential bonding** is described in BS7671 as an electrical connection maintaining various exposed-conductive-parts and extraneous-conductive-parts at substantially the same potential, for the purposes of safety.

b) **Earthing** is defined in BS7671 as the 'connection of the exposed-conductive-parts of an installation to the main earthing terminal of that installation'. Earthing is required on safety Class I devices to enable the protective measure of the automatic disconnection of supply to operate (tripping an overcurrent protective device) should the basic insulation of the Class I device fail.

c) **Earthing for lightning protection** is a connection to earth as part of the lightning protection system (LPS)

d) **Array frame functional earthing** is the connection of the array frame to earth to enable a part of the PV system to function correctly. In general, array frame functional earthing is specified to ensure that the array isolation measures perform correctly. Circumstances of this earthing arrangement can be found in the IET Code of Practice relating to Grid Connected Solar Photovoltaic Systems (5.13.5).

It should be noted that the requirements described in the following diagram apply only to PV arrays constructed using electrically conducting and interconnected metallic frames. The following mounting structures do not require array frame earthing:

● Array mounting structures that are comprised wholly of non-conducting materials (for example, plastic, wood etc.); and

● Array mounting assemblies that use discrete metallic elements (for example, brackets, bolts etc.) in such a manner that there is no electrical path from the frame of one module to another.

To determine if the array frame requires to be earthed or bonded, the following diagram should be consulted:

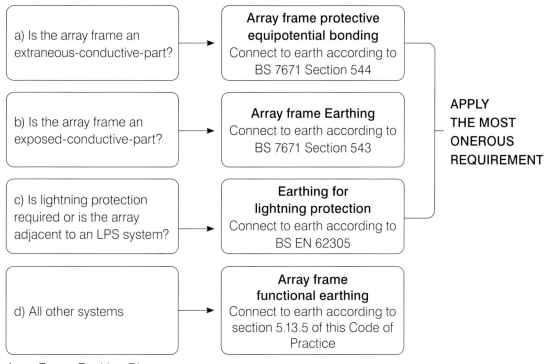

Array Frame Earthing Diagram -
Courtesy of IET Code of Practice for Grid-Connected Solar Photovoltaic Systems

NOTE: Some type of connection between the array frame and earth will be required in all installations IET CoP 2015.

The previous diagram makes reference to the array frame being an exposed-conductive part, an extraneous-conductive part or part of another system. This will influence whether the frame is earthed, bonded or supplied with a functional earth. In order to ascertain which method would be required, an understanding of the terminology used is needed.

BS7671:2018 gives the following definitions:

Exposed Conductive Part: Conductive part of equipment which can be touched and which is not normally live, but which can become live under fault conditions.

Extraneous Conductive Part: A conductive part liable to introduce a potential, generally Earth potential, and not forming part of the electrical installation.

IET BS 7671 Guidance Note 8 Earthing and Bonding offers guidance on determining whether a part is an extraneous conductive part. A resistance test is carried out between the part and the main earthing terminal (MET) and where the value recorded is greater than 22K (most cases) then the part can be considered to be isolated from earth and therefore is not an extraneous conductive part. If the value is less that 22K then the part is an extraneous conductive part and therefore protective equipotential bonding, as required by BS7671:2018, should be applied.

For a typical domestic roof structure the fixing and securing arrangement of the array is likely to be non-conductive materials used in the roof structures and therefore the likelihood of creating extraneous conductive parts through the structure is low.

In commercial and industrial applications where the building structures are largely steelwork the fixings and securing arrangements are likely to provide bonding to the structure and be sufficient to maintain electrical continuity without the need for additional bonding requirements.

For ground mounted installations, it may appear that the frame is an extraneous conductive part, however, further advice may need to be taken. The IET code of practice for grid connected solar photovoltaic systems gives advice on the earthing of ground mounted, accessible array frames.

"Where the PV system is connected to an installation with a TN-C-S (PME) supply AND where the PV array is generally accessible (for example, ground mounted), a local earth electrode shall be provided at the array location. The electrode shall be provided in accordance with BS7671 section 542.2. The electrode shall be bonded to the building's main earthing terminal and also connected to the PV array frame earth."

Further information on this is contained within that code of practice.

RCD

In a grid-connected PV system, there is no fundamental requirement to fit an RCD to the circuit that feeds the inverter(s).

However, in some circumstances, an RCD may be required by BS7671 due to the nature of the circuit (for example, where unprotected cables are buried within a wall at an insufficient depth). In such a case, the selection of the RCD needs to take into account the inverter

Where an RCD is fitted to a circuit that feeds an inverter, the RCD shall be selected as follows:

Table 4.1 – RCD Selection

Scenario	Inverter and Circuit Conditions	RCD Selection
1	All inverters in the circuit include at least simple separation between the AC and DC sides.	RCD selection need not take into account the inverter.
2	All inverters in the circuit include at least simple separation or the inverters, by construction, are not able to feed DC fault currents into the electrical installation.	
3	An inverter in the circuit does not include simple separation and is able to feed DC fault currents into the electrical installation.	Type B RCD required.

RCD Selection Table – Courtesy of IET Code of Practice for Grid-Connected Solar Photovoltaic Systems

An inverter that does not include simple separation (often referred to as a 'transformer-less inverter') may be able to feed a DC fault current into the AC side of the system. This DC element may not be picked up by a conventional RCD and may also hinder it's normal operation. A Type B RCD is, by construction, able to handle and detect both AC and DC residual currents.

Where grid-connected PV systems are fed from an RCD (particularly systems using transformer-less inverters), nuisance tripping of the RCD can be relatively common. Where possible, it is recommended designing a system so that the inverter(s) are not fed from a RCD.

Solar PV systems shall not be installed to the load side of any RCD that is shared with other circuits (e.g. where the RCD is feeding a number of circuit breakers/circuits). This is necessary to ensure the continued safe operation of the RCD, prevent the possibility of a fault on a circuit continuing to be fed by the inverter for up to five seconds after the RCD has tripped and prevent nuisance tripping."

Protection against lightning and overvoltage

When a new structure or system is installed, consideration has to be given to the possible effects caused by either a direct or indirect lightning strike. Both the safety and the protection of life and reliance on the uninterrupted operation of electrical and electronic systems need to be assured. To achieve these goals, it is recommended that the design, installation and testing of the lightning and surge protection systems be carried out by a suitably qualified specialist.

A safe and effective system is dependent on a correct risk assessment being carried out, followed by a fully co-ordinated design and installation. This should take into account the requirements of other disciplines working on the project, especially with regard to the different types of earthing systems that may be specified.

Design and installation of any such systems should be carried out in accordance with BS EN 62305, which is the UK's lightning protection standard.

BS EN 62305 consists of four parts, which are:

- BS EN 62305-1   General principles

- BS EN 62305-2   Risk management

- BS EN 62305-3   Physical damage to structures and life hazard

- BS EN 62305-4   Electrical and electronic systems within structures

Risk assessment

The risk assessment procedure described within the lightning protection standard, BS EN 62305, is used to calculate the actual risk of lighting effects on a specific site/system.

This requires the actual risk value (R) to be compared to a tolerable risk value (RT) to determine if a problem exists. Should the actual risk value exceed the tolerable risk value (RT), a solution will be required which will be determined by the degree of difference between the two.

Action may be required to reduce this risk to an acceptable level. This may require the fitting of an external lightning protection system (LPS), lightning current or surge arresters or a combination of both.

In many cases (for example, for a typical domestic PV installation), there will be no requirement for a dedicated LPS or for any additional surge protection device (SPD) to be fitted. Where it is considered that SPD protection is required, the presence and type of any factory-fitted SPD within an inverter should be checked, as these may prove sufficient. Some inverters may also have the capability to install and additional SPD within them.

Solar PV installations on tall or exposed buildings, or on buildings that already have an LPS fitted, will need particular scrutiny. Installations in open fields and/or with long cable runs will also require similar scrutiny.

Buildings with an LPS already fitted will require the installation of SPD(s) to the PV system – and a specialist should be consulted to advise on the location/type.

External LPS

An external LPS consists of an air termination network, down conductors and earthing system.

Depending on the specific requirements of other aspects on the project, either an equipotentially bonded or an isolated lightning protection system may be specified.

Separation distances need to be calculated and maintained between the lightning protection system, structure and metallic services. An isolated design can be applied to the whole structure or parts of the structure, thus making it an ideal system for roof-mounted PV systems, etc. Isolated lightning conductor systems can prevent the lightning strike from coupling directly to the PV array.

Lightning current and surge arresters

If the risk assessment highlights the need for lightning current and surge protection, Document 4 of the lightning protection standard refers to the correct type and positioning of the devices required. BS EN 62305-4 cross refers to BS EN 50539-11/-12, (Low-voltage surge protection devices. Surge protection devices for specific application including DC. Part 11 Requirements and tests for SPDs in photovoltaic applications; Part 12 Selection and application principles. SPDs connected to photovoltaic installations), which outlines the requirements and testing methods for surge protection devices connected to low-voltage power distribution systems.

An SPD operates by diverting or limiting potentially harmful surge currents. Two types of SPD generally need to be considered:

a) Type 1: Lightning current arrestor designed to discharge very high levels of lightning current.

b) Type 2: Surge arrestor intended to divert lightning induced surges. Used to protect particular components or parts of a system.

When selecting an SPD, it shall have a rating to suit the circuit it is being installed in (voltage rating, AC/DC, etc.)

Combined Type 1-Type 2 arrestors are available and commonly used. There are also SPD's specifically designed for installation on DC PV circuits readily available, where PV combiner boxes come with SPD's pre-fitted.

Fire-fighter switches

It is good practice to install a method of isolating the DC as close to the array as possible. One method of doing this is to install a fire-fighter's switch that will provide isolation of the DC side of the installation from the point where the switch disconnects the circuit.

Whilst the installation of fire-fighter switches is not commonplace at the moment, it is considered very good practice and perhaps provides installers and contractors with a form of competitive advantage in the form of increased safety. The diagram below illustrates such a switch and the motorised actuating device.

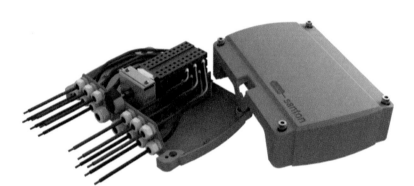 

Source (www.santonswitchgear.com)

Grid connected inverter types

The inverter is one of the key components of a PV system. Not only does this allow us to covert DC to AC, but it also maximises the PV output and provides a safe connection to the grid.

Grid connected inverters are generally connected to PV strings, which supply the DC input and convert to AC single phase, low voltage utility mains transferred to the grid distribution network.

Grid connected inverters connected in the UK are normally sized at 80% of the peak power (Wp) of the PV array. Due to relatively low average solar radiation, we can undersize the inverter to reflect this. When the PV array is operating at peak irradiation (peak PV output), the inverter output power will be limited to it's maximum value. For example, an inverter can have an input power of 3kw but its maximum output power value may only be 2.5kW.

These inverters must also carry an engineering recommendation of the current edition of a EREC G98 type test certificate and comply with all other parts of the current edition of EREC G98 unless specifically agreed by an engineer employed and appointed by the Distribution Network Operator for this purpose and in writing. This Engineering Recommendation will be looked at in detail later in this module.

A key safety feature of inverters, which are compliant with the current edition of EREC G98, is that the PV system will disconnect when the distribution system is not energised. This is to prevent a hazardous situation where the PV system could feed the network or local distribution system during either a planned or unscheduled loss of mains supply. This scenario is termed 'islanding' (which was explained in the previous module) and presents a potential danger to those working on the network/distribution system. The Type Tests carried out through the current edition of EREC G98 ensure that an inverter is properly prevented from such situations.

There are three main types of grid connected inverters. These are:

- Central inverters
- String inverters
- Module inverters

Central inverters

Central inverters are ground mounted and may not require any additional enclosure or housing for installation. The design of the inverter base must be suitable for the weight of the inverter assembly and may need to include ducting to allow for cable entries. Where installed within buildings, care is needed to ensure that the inverter room provides sufficient access around the inverter and adequate ventilation.

Larger central inverters are normally installed within a purpose-built walk-in container that is supplied pre-installed with all the necessary switchgear and wiring assemblies. For open-field arrays, the location of the inverter will need to be selected to suit AC cable routes and at a location to minimise DC cable runs. Due to the large size of central inverters, the location will also need to be chosen to prevent shade from the inverter falling onto the array. Central inverters are not normally chosen for domestic installations.

Mini Central Grid Connect Inverter
(Image courtesy of www.thepowerstore.co.uk)

String inverters

String inverters fall into two types:

- Multiple string inverters.
- Single string inverters.

The theory behind these inverters is to connect one or more PV strings to a single inverter. The system can also be enlarged by having more than one inverter with each one having one or more PV strings also.

String inverters are connected directly to module strings and this provides the following advantages and cost savings compared with central inverter concepts:

Grid Connected String Inverter
(Image courtesy of www.fronius.com)

- Omission of the PV junction box.

- Reduction of the module cabling to series interconnection and omission of the DC main cable.

String inverters can also incorporate DC optimisers. These are module level electrical devices which condition the output of a PV module.

Typically, DC optimisers provide module-level maximum-power point tracking, with the units mounted on the rear of the PV modules or incorporated into the module junction box.

A DC optimiser requires a separate inverter to enable the grid connection. There are two distinct architectures; those that are designed to work with any inverter (providing the inverter meets certain requirements), and those that are designed to work with a specific inverter (usually inverter and optimiser are from the same manufacturer).

Some DC optimisers will work with one module each and others will work with pairs of modules. Some are also able to provide module-level performance monitoring and diagnostics as well as added safety features

Module inverters

Module inverters (also known as microinverters) are fitted to each module in an installation, essentially meaning that each module is its own array. Not only do these inverters offer the same module-level performance monitoring and diagnostics as DC optimisers but they also convert the DC of the module to AC, minimising the DC cabling. This means that all equipment from the array will be AC and may require a bespoke form of AC connection between each inverter. This can be a busbar system, where each inverter is plugged into the busbar and a single connection from the busbar taken to a junction box or circuit breaker/RCBO.

This type of system has many of the advantages of a string inverter using DC optimisers, where each module can be monitored and any shaded modules won't affect the performance of those that are unshaded. However, module inverter systems tend to be more expensive, due to the number of inverters to be installed and if the inverter requires to be repaired/replaced, it can be much more difficult to access this than an inverter mounted inside the building.

Inverter standards

All inverters shall comply with the requirements of BS EN 62109 – Safety of power converters for use in photovoltaic power systems or BS EN 50178 – Electronic equipment for use in power installations and shall carry a CE mark.

Inverter sizing

The sizing of a grid connected inverter is influenced by a number of factors, including:

- The inverters ability for use in the UK (G98/99 compliant)

- The MPP (Maximum Power Point) voltage range of the inverter

- The desired inverter-array power ratio

Inverter matching is generally performed using software packages that each inverter manufacturer make available. For any combination of modules and inverter, the software allows the system designer to ensure that the array output will remain within the inverter's peak and MPP voltage ranges for a pre-set range of conditions – including, most significantly, the cell temperature range.

Variations in cell temperature will affect the array voltage considerably. It is important to consider both high and low array-temperature operation:

- At low cell temperatures, the array voltage will rise. It is important to ensure that the maximum array voltage remains below the inverter maximum voltage rating. This can be calculated using the temperature coefficient formulae discussed in module 2 relating to V_{OC} STC at -15°C.

- At high cell temperatures, the array voltage will fall. The impact of this low voltage needs to be considered with respect to inverter operation and MPP voltage range. If the voltage were to fall below MPP voltage range, the inverter would fail to optimise the output of the array and may not produce any output at all.

It should be noted that inverters shall be suitable for the voltage maxima (VDC-MAX) calculated for the circuit which it is connected to. For systems with DC optimisers installed, the optimisers shall be rated for the voltage and current maxima of both the module and the string into which they are assembled.

Temperature and MPP voltage range

An inverter must be selected to safely withstand the maximum array voltage and current. This must include any overvoltage period which is a feature of some module types. This must also include verification that the inverter can safely withstand the array open circuit voltage (VOC) at -15OC. By ensuring that the inverter is capable of withstanding the VDC-MAX value calculated for the PV array, this will satisfy the operation of the inverter when the array is at this temperature.

Not only must the inverter be able to safely withstand a PV array operation between extremes of temperature (-15°C to 80°C) but it must also ensure that the PV array stays within the MPP voltage range of the inverter under normal operating conditions. If the array moves outside of this voltage range, losses will occur.

It is permissible for a narrower temperature band (-10°C to 70°C) to be used when looking at the operational range of an inverter. In such cases, an assessment should be made as to the temperature range acceptable and appropriate for that particular site and array installation type – for example, a building-integrated module can be expected to reach higher cell temperatures than a module mounted on an open frame in a field."

Power ratio

Grid connected inverters in the UK are typically sized between 80-110% of the peak power of the PV array. However, most systems are specified with an inverter power rating which is smaller than the array power, known as under sizing. This is mainly due to PV modules in the UK operating below their nominal rated power for much of the time because of average solar radiation values and not meeting the STC values. If the PV array was to receive STC values during its operation, which would mean that the array is producing peak output, then the undersized inverter would 'clip' the output power produced.

Reasons for under sizing the inverter also include:

- Inverter efficiency is generally lower when operating at low power levels. Under sizing of an inverter can decrease losses at times of normal irradiance levels,

- The array is sited in a sub-optimal location, orientation or pitch and as such is expected to produce a lower than normal output,

- The annual yield may not justify the extra cost of a larger inverter,

- When a grid connection limit is imposed on a site, it may be beneficial to undersize the inverter to gain maximum generation. An example could be an inverter which is limited to 3.68kW (as per G98) but is connected to a larger array (between 5-6kW) where the array is able to produce more power in sub-optimal conditions, Manufacturers should always be consulted on the maximum undersizing possible.

There are also situations where oversizing the inverter can be considered, including:

- Limited inverter selection (not common),

- May increase inverter lifespan,

- The array is expected to produce significant power – for example, an array on a solar tracker."

Inverter ventilation

Inverters' generate heat and should be provided with sufficient ventilation. Clearance distances as specified by the manufacturer (e.g. to a heat sink) should also be observed. Inverter locations such as plant or boiler rooms, or roof spaces prone to high temperatures, should be carefully considered to avoid overheating.

Failure to follow this can cause a loss in system performance as the inverter will de-rate when it reaches its maximum operating temperature. This should be highlighted within the operation and use manual, left with the customer and ideally with a label – "not to block ventilation" – placed next to the inverter.

It is recommended that Inverters carry a sign 'Inverter – isolate AC and DC before carrying out work'.

Similar to over and under voltage, over and under current requires careful design and inverter characteristic matching. Under current may render the system inoperable if there is insufficient input current for the system and by using the correct design procedures in terms of short circuit current then the system provides over current DC protection.

Inverters that comply with ENA Engineering Recommendation current edition of EREC G98 criteria provide protection against AC over and under voltage, over and under frequency. These operating parameters are listed in Module 3. Overcurrent protection should be provided, in accordance with the current edition of BS 7671 at the point of distribution (distribution board or consumer unit) in the form of a circuit breaker or RCBO.

Where a system features multiple strings/arrays with significantly different orientation or inclination, the strings/arrays should be connected to an inverter with a multiple MPPT function or separate inverters should be utilised. This is only required where the variations in orientation or inclination are such that connecting the strings/arrays to a single MPPT input may significantly reduce the overall performance of the system.

Typical PV array and inverter sizing

To ensure that the PV system is efficient and the inverter is capable of operating properly. An inverter requires a certain amount of voltage and current to operate and keep the MPP within range. Below is a typical example of a domestic installation and the equipment that would be selected for the installation.

Example

Consider a 3kWp array composed of 12 x 250Wp PV modules arranged in 2 parallel strings of 6 series-connected modules. An inverter of 2500W would be appropriate, i.e. an under-sizing ratio of 0.83 (83%). There are no DC optimisers fitted to this system. It is important that the expected operating voltage of the PV is within the allowable limits of the inverter as stated on the data sheet.

Module Specification

The following values have been taken from the module data sheet.

At STC, the following values are:

- Open-Circuit Voltage (V_{OC}) – 38.5V

- Short-Circuit Current (I_{SC}) – 7.4A

At STC, the following values are:

- Peak Power Voltage (V_{MP}) – 36.2V

- Peak Power Current (I_{MP}) – 6.91A

Inverter Specification

The following values have been taken from the inverter data sheet.

- Maximum DC Voltage – 400V

- Maximum DC Power – 3450W

- MPPT Operating Voltage – 150-400V

- Maximum Input Current – 19A

From these values, the ratings of the equipment can be calculated along with the array characteristics.

String Open-Circuit Voltage – No of modules x Open-Circuit Voltage (V_{OC})

6 x 38.5 = **231V**

Array Short-Circuit Current – No of strings x Short-Circuit Current (I_{SC})

2 x 7.4 = **14.8A**

These two calculations are very important as they go partly towards proving that the inverter will be able to withstand the maximum values of both voltage and current from the array. However, it should be noted that these calculated values are not the array voltage or current maxima. In order to ensure that the inverter is able to safely withstand variations in irradiance and temperature, the multiplier for crystalline modules must be applied

Therefore:

Maximum Voltage (V_{DC-MAX}) – String Open-Circuit Voltage x 1.15

231 x 1.15 = **265.5V**

Maximum Current (I_{DC-MAX}) – Array Short-Circuit Current x 1.25

14.8 x 1.25 = **18.5A**

Any inverter selected for this system should be capable of accepting the values of voltage and current above.

The values to be calculated next are the MPP voltage and current. This will give a peak power output value.

String MPP Voltage – No of modules x Peak Power Voltage (V_{MP})

6 x 36.2 = **217.2V**

The characteristics of the inverter show that it will track the MPP between the voltages of 150-400V. The MPP voltage value must fall in between these two figures.

Array MPP Current – No of strings x Peak Power Current (I_{MP})

2 x 6.91 = **13.8A**

Now that both the MPP voltage and current values for the array have been calculated, the peak power output of the array must be considered.

Peak Power Output – String MPP Voltage x Array MPP Current

$217.2 \times 13.8 =$ **2997.36W**

Again, this value must be less than the inverters' maximum DC power value. The selected inverters' maximum DC power input is 3450W, so our calculation is acceptable.

The results of the calculations indicate that the inverter is correctly sized for the size and configuration of the PV array. The string cabling and the DC array isolator must now be sized. Using the calculations that were used in the component rating section, the sizing of both can be determined.

Module String Cabling – Current Rating:

ISC STC x (N-1) x 1.25 (where N is the number of parallel connected strings)

$7.4 \times (2-1) \times 1.25 =$ **9.25A**

PV Array Switch Dis-Connector – Current Rating:

Array Short-Circuit Current x 1.25

$14.8 \times 1.25 =$ **18.5A** (I_{DC-MAX})

PV String/Array Switch Dis-connector – Voltage Rating:

String Open-Circuit Voltage x 1.15

$231 \times 1.15 =$ **265.5V** (V_{DC-MAX})

These figures are used to purchase the appropriate rated equipment that will be required for the operation and maintenance of the PV system.

The example above stipulated the quantity and arrangement of the PV array. In the example on the next page, the size of roof space that is available is considered and a PV system sized accordingly.

Array Sizing

When looking at starting to design a PV system, one of the most important factors, with the exception of cost, is the size of the area where the array will be sited. For most installations, this would be a house roof. Not only will this dictate how many panels that can be fitted but may also decide the orientation of the array.

Example

A client has asked for a quote for a PV installation on their roof. They have no set budget and so can afford to put up as many modules as will fit. If the roof area is 6.5m x 6.5m and the specific module to be used has dimensions of 1.45m tall x 0.66m wide, leaving a 10mm wide gap between rows, 5mm between each module and a measurement of 500mm from all edges, how many panels can be fitted on the roof?

This is a very simple calculation, as the available roof area should be considered first. The question indicates that there be a 500mm space available at all edges of the roof. Therefore, this should be subtracted from the roof dimensions:

6.5m – 1000mm (500mm x 2) = **5.5m**

The result (5.5m) would be for both the height and the width of the roof, as the roof requires a 500mm space from all edges. Now that the available height and width have been calculated, these dimensions can be used to calculate how many panels can be fitted on the roof. If the modules were to be mounted in a **portrait orientation**, the number of rows (or strings) to be installed can be calculated:

$$5.5m / 1.45m = \textbf{3.79 rows}$$

Now that the number of rows has been calculated, the spacing between the rows should be considered. The spacing between the rows is 10mm; therefore, this should be subtracted from the dimension that was calculated previously. If there are three rows, then there are only two 'gaps' between the rows.

$$5.5m - 20mm (10mm \times 2) / 1.45m = \textbf{3.77 rows}$$

This would still allow three rows of panels to be installed.

The same calculations must be carried out for the number of modules in each row. This time, instead of using the height dimension of the module, the width must be used.

$$5.5m / 0.66m = \textbf{8.33 modules}$$

0.9 of a panel cannot be installed, so this figure would be rounded down to 8 panels. The horizontal spacing should now be subtracted from this calculation:

$$5.5m - 35mm (5mm \times 7) / 0.66m = \textbf{8.2 modules}$$

The following array pattern can now be used:

Rows of modules – 3

No of modules in each row – 8

Total No of modules – 3 x 8 = **24 modules**

This gives the maximum number of modules that can be fitted to this roof.

The client has now notified the installer to say that he has had to cut his budget and can only afford 12 modules to be fitted. Using the data below, calculate the array's total power output, I_{SC} & I_{MP} and the string V_{OC} & V_{MP}.

Module Characteristics

MPP Power Output – 300w

Short-Circuit Current (I_{SC}) – 9.2A

Peak Power Current (I_{MP}) – 7.79A

Open-Circuit Voltage (V_{OC}) – 41.4V

Peak Power Voltage (V_{MP}) – 38.5V

To calculate the arrays total power output, the MPP Power Output value must be multiplied by the number of modules that will be installed.

$$300w \times 12 = \textbf{3600w}$$

An ideal layout for the array would be 2 rows (or strings) of 6 modules.

The array's Open-Circuit Voltage and Peak Power Voltage:

$$\text{Array } V_{OC} - 6 \times 41.4 = \mathbf{248.4V}$$

$$\text{Array } V_{MP} - 6 \times 38.5 = \mathbf{231V}$$

The array's Short-Circuit Current and Peak Power Current:

$$\text{Array } I_{SC} - 2 \times 9.2 = \mathbf{18.4A}$$

$$\text{Array } I_{MP} - 2 \times 7.79 = \mathbf{15.6A}$$

The maximum values of voltage and current must also be calculated to ensure that the inverter is capable of withstanding these values.

Maximum voltage of the array:

$$\text{Array Max Voltage } (V_{DC\text{-}MAX}) - 248.4 \times 1.15 = \mathbf{285.7V}$$

Maximum current of the array:

$$\text{Array Max Current } (I_{DC\text{-}MAX}) - 18.4 \times 1.25 = \mathbf{23A}$$

Now that these details have been calculated, this will dictate which inverter can be used.

The client has looked at two inverters and has asked for the installer's help in choosing which one should be installed. Given the data below, decide which inverter would be chosen and give reasons why.

Inverter Characteristics

	Inverter 1	Inverter 2
Input Voltage	100-300V	275-500V
Input Current	12A	25A
Input Power	1200-1900Wp	3800-4500Wp

In order to ensure that the inverter will operate normally, it has to be able to work in the ranges of the values that were calculated earlier.

Inverter 2 cannot be used due to that lack of voltage and power being produced by the array. This only allows inverter 1 to be used but even then, the characteristics of that inverter must be looked at closely.

The inverter will operate in the range of voltage that the array will provide but it cannot accept the amount of total power from the array. In this case, 2 x inverter 1 should be used, that is to say each string will be connected to its own inverter. This will satisfy all the characteristics required for inverter 1 to operate, including the maximum input current, where 23A would half as only one string is connected to each inverter. Different inverters will have different characteristics, and all of these must be met for the inverter to operate properly. Again, different array arrangements will give different characteristics, but the output power will always remain the same.

This is a simple process whereby the budget and roof (or mounting site) dictates how large a PV system will be.

Array and Inverter Sizing Exercises

Using the table overleaf, answer the following questions.

1) A gable sloped roof has dimensions on one face of 8m (width) x 7.3m (height). From the data given for module 1, how many modules (fitted in portrait orientation) can be used in the array? If the number of modules were reduced to 16, what would the array arrangement be and which of the inverters listed would be chosen and why?

> Maximum spacing between each module   5mm
>
> Maximum spacing between each row   10mm
>
> Minimum spacing from all edges   **500mm**

2) Using the same roof dimensions and spacing's in question 1, what differences would occur to the PV system if module 4 were to be used? If the number of modules were reduced to 20, would this have a greater power output than question 1?

3) A gable sloped roof has dimensions on one face of 10.2m (width) x 6.3m (height). From the data given in the table, how many modules (fitted in portrait orientation) can be used in the array for module types 2 & 3? The client has asked that their PV system give them the greatest power output possible. Which of the two modules would you choose and why? Which inverter would be appropriate for your choice?

> Maximum spacing between each module   5mm
>
> Maximum spacing between each row   10mm
>
> Minimum spacing from all edges   **500mm**

Module Characteristics and Dimensions

	Dimensions (H x W in m)	Max Power Output	Open-Circuit Voltage	Short-Circuit Current	Max Peak Voltage	Max Peak Current
Module 1	1.8 x 0.72	240W	34.5V	8.7A	32.3V	7.4A
Module 2	1.65 x 0.69	200W	32.6V	7.7A	29.5V	6.8A
Module 3	1.73 x 0.77	275W	39.1V	8.9A	36.7V	7.5A
Module 4	1.32 x 0.54	195W	30.3V	8.8A	26.1V	7.5A

Inverter Characteristics

	Input Voltage	Max Input Voltage	Input Power	Max Input Current
Inverter 1	240V-330V	400V	3500W-4500W	23A
Inverter 2	320V-440V	500V	4000W-5600W	32A
Inverter 3	210V-290V	320V	3100W-3900W	20A

Array and Inverter Sizing Exercises

Answers

1. **Available roof area**

   8m – 1000mm = **7m** width of the roof

   7.3m – 1000mm = **6.3m** height of the roof

   Number of rows (Strings)

   6.3m / 1.8m = **3.5 rows**   (3 rows)

   Number of modules

   7m / 0.72 = **9.7 modules**   (9 modules)

   Number of rows including spacing

   (6.3m – 20mm) / 1.8m = **3.4 rows**   (3 rows)

   Number of modules including spacing

   (7m – 45mm) / 0.72m = **9.6 modules**   (9 modules)

   Total No of modules

   9 modules x 3 rows = **27 modules**

   The number of modules is limited to 16. This gives the array 2 strings having 8 modules each.

   Total Power Output for the Array

   16 modules x 240W = **3,840W**

   The Array's Short-Circuit Current and Peak Power Current

   Array ISC – 2 x 8.7A = **17.4A**

   Array IMP – 2 x 7.4A = **14.8A**

   The Array's Open-Circuit Voltage and Peak Power Voltage

   Array VOC – 8 x 34.5V = **276V**

   Array VMP – 8 x 32.3V = **258.4V**

   Based on the calculations for question 1, only **Inverter 1** can be installed.

Array and Inverter Sizing Exercises

Answers

2. **Available roof area**

8m – 1000mm = **7m** width of the roof

7.3m – 1000mm = **6.3m** height of the roof

Number of rows (Strings)

6.3m / 1.32m = **4.77 rows**   (4 rows)

Number of modules

7m / 0.54 = **12.9 modules**   (12 modules)

Number of rows including spacing

(6.3m – 30mm) / 1.32m = **4.75 rows**   (4 rows)

Number of modules including spacing

(7m – 55mm) / 0.54m = **12.8 modules**   (12 modules)

Total No of modules

12 modules x 4 rows = **48 modules**

The number of modules is limited to 20.

Total Power Output for the Array

20 modules x 195W = **3,900W**

The power output from this array is **greater** than that in question 1.

Array and Inverter Sizing Exercises

Answers

3. **Available roof area**

10.2m – 1000mm = **9.2m** width of the roof

6.3m – 1000mm = **5.3m** height of the roof

Module 2 Calculations

Number of rows (Strings)

5.3m / 1.65m = **3.21 rows**   (3 rows)

Number of modules

9.2m / 0.69m = **13.3 modules**   (13 modules)

Number of rows including spacing

(5.3m – 20mm) / 1.65m = **3.2 rows**   (3 rows)

Number of modules including spacing

(9.2m – 60mm) / 0.69m = **13.2 modules**   (13 modules)

Total No of modules

13 modules x 3 rows = **39 modules**

Total Power Output for the Array

39 modules x 200W = **7,800W**

If all the available space on the roof were to be used and 39 modules installed, this would give the following calculations:

The Array's Short-Circuit Current and Peak Power Current

Array ISC – 3 x 7.7A = **23.1A**

Array IMP – 3 x 6.8A = **20.4A**

The Array's Open-Circuit Voltage and Peak Power Voltage

Array VOC – 13 x 32.6V = **423.8V**

Array VMP – 13 x 29.5V = **383.5V**

Array and Inverter Sizing Exercises

Answers

Module 3 Calculations

Number of rows (Strings)

5.3m / 1.73m = **3.06 rows**   (3 rows)

Number of modules

9.2m / 0.77m = **11.9 modules**   (11 modules)

Number of rows including spacing

(5.3m – 20mm) / 1.73m = **3.05 rows**   (3 rows)

Number of modules including spacing

(9.2m – 50mm) / 0.77m = **11.8 modules**   (11 modules)

Total No of modules

11 modules x 3 rows = **33 modules**

Total Power Output for the Array

33 modules x 275W = **9,075W**

If all the available space on the roof were to be used and 33 modules installed, this would give the following calculations:

The Array's Short-Circuit Current and Peak Power Current

Array I_{SC} – 3 x 8.9A = **26.7A**

Array I_{MP} – 3 x 7.5A = **22.5A**

The Array's Open-Circuit Voltage and Peak Power Voltage

Array V_{OC} – 11 x 39.1V = **430.1V**

Array V_{MP} – 11 x 36.7V = **403.7V**

If the client is looking for the greatest power output, module 3 should be used. Unfortunately, the inverters available (in the table) don't have the capability to be connected to such a large array. Therefore, an inverter with the appropriate characteristics would have to be sought.

System performance calculations

As was discussed in Module 2, the performance of a PV system is dependent on a number of factors, namely:

- Array orientation and inclination

- Shade effects

- Temperature effects

As well as the factors above, there are additional factors which need to be looked at. These are:

- Geographical location (see the attached postcode chart)

- Daily and annual variation (irradiance)

- Other factors which include:

  - Panel characteristics and manufacturing tolerances

  - Inverter efficiency

  - Inverter – array matching

  - Cable losses

  - Soiling of the array

  - Grid availability

  - Equipment availability

As part of the quotation process, the client must be given an estimate of the annual electricity generated by the PV system in kWh/year (AC). This is determined using the following formula:

$$\text{Annual AC output (kWh)} = \text{kWp} \times \text{Kk} \times \text{SF}$$

Where:

- kWp refers to the kWp output of the system. This will have been calculated at the design stage of the PV system.

- Kk is a tabulated value of kWh/kWp for different postcode zones. These tables have 1° increments for inclination and 5° increments for orientation.

- SF relates to a shade factor that needs to be determined by the installer/designer.

kWh/kWp value (Kk)

The following map and table give information on the postcode zone relating to the location of the PV system. Each zone has a table from which the Kk value can be obtained. This value will alter depending upon the orientation and inclination of the PV array.

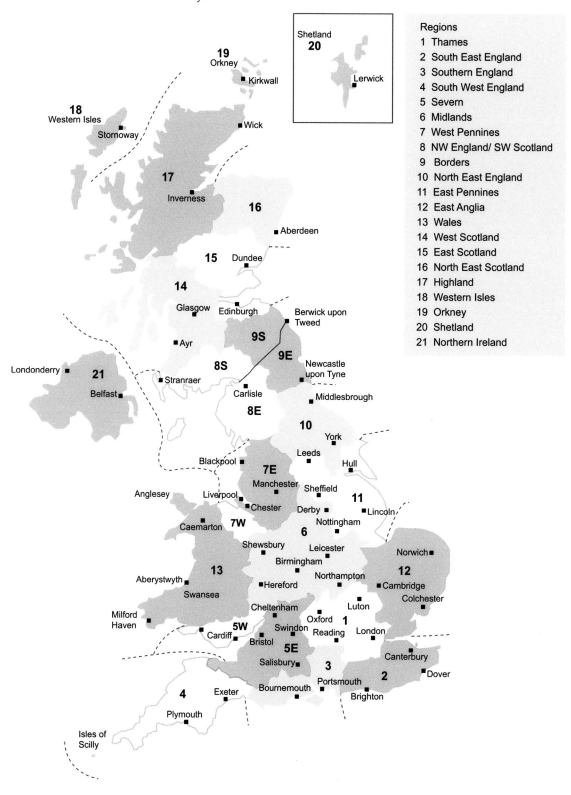

From the MCS guide to installation of PV systems

Postcode	Zone	Postcode	Zone	Postcode	Zone	Postcode	Zone
AB	16	FY	7E	ML	14	SK13	6
AL	1	G	14	N	1	SK17	6
B	6	GL	5E	NE	9E	SK22-23	6
BA	5E	GU	1	NG	11	SL	1
BB	7E	GU11-12	3	NN	6	SM	1
BD	11	GU14	3	NP	5W	SN	5E
BD23-24	10	GU28-29	2	NPS	13	SN7	1
BH	3	GU30-35	3	NR	12	SO	3
BL	7E	GU46	3	NW	1	SP	5E
BN	2	GU51-52	3	OL	7E	SP6-11	3
BR	2	HA	1	OX	1	SR	9E
BS	5E	HD	11	PA	14	SR7-8	10
BT	21	HG	10	PE	12	SS	12
CA	8E	HP	1	PE9-12	11	ST	6
CB	12	HR	6	PE20-25	11	SW	1
CF	5W	HS	18	PH	15	SY	6
CH	7E	HU	11	PH19-25	17	SY14	7E
CH5-8	7W	HX	11	PH26	16	SY15-25	13
CM	12	IG	12	PH30-44	17	TA	5E
CM21-23	1	IP	12	PH49	14	TD	9S
CO	12	IV	17	PH50	14	TD12	9E
CR	1	IV30-32	16	PL	4	TD15	9E
CT	2	IV36	16	PO	3	TF	6
CV	6	KA	14	PO18-22	2	TN	2
CW	7E	KT	1	PR	7E	TQ	4
DA	2	KW	17	RG	1	TR	4
DD	15	KW15-17	19	RG21-29	3	TS	10
DE	6	KY	15	RH	1	TW	1
DG	8S	L	7E	RH10-20	2	UB	1
DH	10	LA	7E	RH77	2	W	1
DH4-5	9E	LA7-23	8E	RM	12	WA	7E
DL	10	LD	13	S	11	WC	1
DN	11	LE	6	S18	6	WD	1
DT	3	LL	7W	S32-33	6	WF	11
DY	6	LL23-27	13	S40-45	6	WN	7E
E	1	LL30-78	13	S49	6	WR	6
EC	1	LN	11	SA	5W	WS	6
EH	15	LS	11	SA14-20	13	WV	6
EH43-46	9S	LS24	10	SA31-48	13	YO	10
EN	1	LU	1	SA61-73	13	YO15-16	11
EN9	12	M	7E	SE	1	YO25	11
EX	4	ME	2	SG	1	ZE	20
FK	14	MK	1	SK	7E		

From the MCS guide to installation of PV systems

Each zone has its own unique table of values for Kk. These are as follows:

Zone 1

Inclination (variation from horizontal)	Orientation (variation from south)									
	0	**5**	**10**	**15**	**20**	**25**	**30**	**35**	**40**	**45**
0	828	828	828	828	828	828	828	828	828	828
1	835	835	835	835	835	835	834	834	833	833
2	843	843	843	842	842	841	841	840	839	838
3	850	850	850	849	849	848	847	846	845	843
4	857	857	857	856	855	854	853	852	850	848
5	864	864	864	863	862	861	859	857	855	853
6	871	871	870	869	868	867	865	863	861	858
7	878	877	877	876	874	873	871	868	866	862
8	884	884	883	882	880	879	876	873	870	867
9	890	890	889	888	886	884	882	878	875	871
10	896	896	895	894	892	890	887	883	880	875
11	902	902	901	900	898	895	892	888	884	879
12	908	908	907	905	903	900	897	893	888	883
13	914	913	912	910	908	905	901	897	892	887
14	919	919	917	916	913	910	906	901	896	890
15	924	924	922	920	918	914	910	905	900	894
16	929	929	927	925	922	919	914	909	903	897
17	934	933	932	930	927	923	918	913	907	900
18	938	938	936	934	931	927	922	917	910	903
19	943	942	941	938	935	931	926	920	913	906
20	947	946	945	942	939	935	929	923	916	908
21	951	950	949	946	943	938	933	926	919	911
22	954	954	952	950	946	941	936	929	922	913
23	958	957	956	953	949	944	939	932	924	915
24	961	961	959	956	952	947	941	934	926	917
25	964	964	962	959	955	950	944	937	928	919
26	967	967	965	962	958	953	946	939	930	921
27	970	969	968	965	960	955	948	941	932	922
28	972	972	970	967	962	957	950	942	933	923
29	975	974	972	969	964	959	952	944	935	924
30	977	976	974	971	966	960	953	945	936	925
31	979	978	976	973	968	962	955	946	937	926
32	980	979	977	974	969	963	956	947	937	926
33	982	981	979	975	970	964	957	948	938	927
34	983	982	980	976	971	965	957	948	938	927
35	984	983	981	977	972	966	958	949	938	927
36	984	984	981	978	973	966	958	949	938	927
37	985	984	982	978	973	966	958	949	938	926
38	985	984	982	978	973	966	958	949	938	925
39	985	984	982	978	973	966	958	948	937	925
40	985	984	982	978	973	966	957	947	936	924
41	984	984	981	977	972	965	956	946	935	922
42	984	983	981	977	971	964	955	945	934	921
43	983	982	980	976	970	963	954	944	932	919
44	982	981	979	975	969	962	953	943	931	918
45	980	980	977	973	967	960	951	941	929	916

Zone 2

		Orientation (variation East or West from South)									
		0	5	10	15	20	25	30	35	40	45
	0	938	938	938	938	938	938	938	938	938	938
	1	947	947	947	946	946	946	945	945	944	944
	2	956	956	956	955	955	954	953	952	951	950
	3	965	965	964	964	963	962	961	960	958	957
	4	974	973	973	972	971	970	969	967	965	963
	5	982	982	981	981	979	978	976	974	971	969
	6	990	990	990	989	987	985	983	980	978	974
	7	999	998	998	996	995	993	990	987	984	980
	8	1006	1006	1005	1004	1002	1000	997	993	989	985
	9	1014	1014	1013	1011	1009	1007	1003	1000	995	990
	10	1022	1021	1020	1019	1016	1013	1010	1006	1001	996
	11	1029	1029	1027	1026	1023	1020	1016	1011	1006	1000
	12	1036	1035	1034	1032	1030	1026	1022	1017	1011	1005
	13	1043	1042	1041	1039	1036	1032	1028	1022	1016	1010
	14	1049	1049	1047	1045	1042	1038	1033	1028	1021	1014
	15	1056	1055	1054	1051	1048	1044	1039	1033	1026	1018
	16	1062	1061	1060	1057	1054	1049	1044	1037	1030	1022
	17	1068	1067	1065	1063	1059	1054	1049	1042	1035	1026
	18	1073	1073	1071	1068	1064	1059	1053	1046	1038	1030
	19	1078	1078	1076	1073	1069	1064	1058	1051	1042	1033
	20	1084	1083	1081	1078	1074	1069	1062	1055	1046	1036
	21	1088	1088	1086	1083	1079	1073	1066	1058	1049	1039
	22	1093	1092	1090	1087	1083	1077	1070	1062	1053	1042
	23	1097	1097	1095	1091	1087	1081	1074	1065	1056	1045
	24	1102	1101	1099	1095	1091	1084	1077	1068	1058	1047
	25	1105	1105	1103	1099	1094	1088	1080	1071	1061	1050
	26	1109	1108	1106	1103	1097	1091	1083	1074	1063	1052
	27	1112	1112	1109	1106	1101	1094	1086	1076	1066	1053
	28	1115	1115	1112	1109	1103	1096	1088	1078	1067	1055
	29	1118	1118	1115	1111	1106	1099	1090	1081	1069	1057
	30	1121	1120	1118	1114	1108	1101	1092	1082	1071	1058
	31	1123	1122	1120	1116	1110	1103	1094	1084	1072	1059
	32	1125	1124	1122	1118	1112	1105	1096	1085	1073	1060
	33	1127	1126	1124	1119	1114	1106	1097	1086	1074	1060
	34	1128	1128	1125	1121	1115	1107	1098	1087	1074	1060
	35	1130	1129	1126	1122	1116	1108	1098	1087	1075	1060
	36	1131	1130	1127	1123	1117	1109	1099	1088	1075	1061
	37	1131	1130	1128	1123	1117	1109	1099	1088	1075	1060
	38	1132	1131	1128	1124	1117	1109	1099	1088	1074	1059
	39	1132	1131	1128	1124	1117	1109	1099	1087	1074	1059
	40	1132	1131	1128	1123	1117	1109	1099	1087	1073	1058
	41	1131	1130	1128	1123	1116	1108	1098	1086	1072	1057
	42	1131	1130	1127	1122	1116	1107	1097	1085	1070	1055
	43	1130	1129	1126	1121	1114	1106	1095	1083	1069	1053
	44	1128	1127	1125	1120	1113	1104	1094	1081	1067	1051
	45	1127	1126	1123	1118	1111	1103	1092	1080	1065	1049

Inclination (variation from horizontal)

Zone 3

	Orientation (variation East or West from South)									
	0	**5**	**10**	**15**	**20**	**25**	**30**	**35**	**40**	**45**
0	857	857	857	857	857	857	857	857	857	857
1	865	865	864	864	864	864	864	863	863	862
2	872	872	872	872	872	871	870	870	869	868
3	880	880	880	879	879	878	877	876	875	873
4	888	888	887	887	886	885	883	882	880	878
5	895	895	894	894	893	891	890	888	886	884
6	902	902	901	901	899	898	896	894	891	888
7	909	909	908	907	906	904	902	899	897	893
8	916	916	915	914	912	910	908	905	902	898
9	923	922	922	920	918	916	913	910	907	902
10	929	929	928	926	924	922	919	915	911	907
11	935	935	934	932	930	928	924	920	916	911
12	941	941	940	938	936	933	929	925	920	915
13	947	947	946	944	941	938	934	930	925	919
14	953	952	951	949	947	943	939	934	929	923
15	958	958	956	954	952	948	944	939	933	926
16	963	963	962	959	956	953	948	943	937	930
17	968	968	967	964	961	957	952	947	940	933
18	973	973	971	969	966	961	956	950	944	936
19	978	977	976	973	970	966	960	954	947	939
20	982	982	980	977	974	969	964	957	950	942
21	986	986	984	981	978	973	967	961	953	944
22	990	990	988	985	981	977	971	964	956	947
23	994	993	992	989	985	980	974	966	958	949
24	997	997	995	992	988	983	977	969	961	951
25	1001	1000	998	995	991	986	979	972	963	953
26	1004	1003	1001	998	994	988	982	974	965	955
27	1007	1006	1004	1001	996	991	984	976	967	956
28	1009	1009	1007	1003	999	993	986	978	968	958
29	1012	1011	1009	1006	1001	995	988	979	970	959
30	1014	1013	1011	1008	1003	997	989	981	971	960
31	1016	1015	1013	1009	1005	998	991	982	972	961
32	1017	1017	1015	1011	1006	1000	992	983	973	961
33	1019	1018	1016	1012	1007	1001	993	984	973	961
34	1020	1019	1017	1013	1008	1002	994	984	974	962
35	1021	1020	1018	1014	1009	1002	994	985	974	962
36	1022	1021	1019	1015	1010	1003	995	985	974	962
37	1022	1022	1019	1015	1010	1003	995	985	974	961
38	1023	1022	1019	1016	1010	1003	995	985	973	960
39	1023	1022	1020	1016	1010	1003	994	984	973	960
40	1023	1022	1019	1015	1010	1002	994	983	972	959
41	1022	1021	1019	1015	1009	1002	993	983	971	957
42	1021	1021	1018	1014	1008	1001	992	981	969	956
43	1020	1020	1017	1013	1007	1000	991	980	968	954
44	1019	1018	1016	1012	1006	998	989	979	966	953
45	1018	1017	1015	1010	1004	997	988	977	964	951

Inclination (variation from horizontal)

Zone 4

		Orientation (variation East or West from South)								
		0	**5**	**10**	**15**	**20**	**25**	**30**	**35**	**40**	**45**
0	907	907	907	907	907	907	907	907	907	907
1	916	916	916	915	915	915	914	914	914	913
2	924	924	924	924	923	923	922	921	920	919
3	933	933	933	932	931	930	929	928	927	925
4	941	941	941	940	939	938	937	935	933	931
5	949	949	949	948	947	945	944	942	939	937
6	957	957	957	956	954	953	950	948	945	942
7	965	965	964	963	962	960	957	954	951	948
8	973	972	972	970	969	966	964	961	957	953
9	980	980	979	977	976	973	970	966	962	958
10	987	987	986	984	982	979	976	972	968	963
11	994	994	993	991	989	986	982	978	973	968
12	1001	1000	999	998	995	992	988	983	978	972
13	1007	1007	1006	1004	1001	998	993	988	983	977
14	1014	1013	1012	1010	1007	1003	999	994	988	981
15	1020	1019	1018	1016	1013	1009	1004	998	992	985
16	1025	1025	1024	1021	1018	1014	1009	1003	996	989
17	1031	1031	1029	1027	1023	1019	1014	1007	1001	993
18	1036	1036	1034	1032	1028	1024	1018	1012	1004	996
19	1041	1041	1039	1037	1033	1028	1023	1016	1008	1000
20	1046	1046	1044	1041	1038	1033	1027	1020	1012	1003
21	1051	1050	1049	1046	1042	1037	1031	1023	1015	1006
22	1055	1055	1053	1050	1046	1041	1034	1027	1018	1009
23	1060	1059	1057	1054	1050	1044	1038	1030	1021	1011
24	1064	1063	1061	1058	1054	1048	1041	1033	1024	1014
25	1067	1067	1065	1062	1057	1051	1044	1036	1027	1016
26	1071	1070	1068	1065	1060	1054	1047	1039	1029	1018
27	1074	1073	1071	1068	1063	1057	1050	1041	1031	1020
28	1077	1076	1074	1071	1066	1060	1052	1043	1033	1022
29	1080	1079	1077	1073	1068	1062	1054	1045	1035	1023
30	1082	1081	1079	1076	1071	1064	1056	1047	1036	1025
31	1084	1084	1081	1078	1073	1066	1058	1048	1038	1026
32	1086	1086	1083	1080	1074	1068	1059	1050	1039	1027
33	1088	1087	1085	1081	1076	1069	1061	1051	1040	1027
34	1089	1089	1086	1082	1077	1070	1062	1052	1040	1027
35	1091	1090	1087	1084	1078	1071	1062	1052	1041	1028
36	1091	1091	1088	1084	1079	1072	1063	1053	1041	1028
37	1092	1091	1089	1085	1079	1072	1063	1053	1041	1027
38	1093	1092	1089	1085	1080	1072	1063	1053	1041	1027
39	1093	1092	1089	1085	1080	1072	1063	1052	1040	1026
40	1093	1092	1089	1085	1079	1072	1063	1052	1039	1025
41	1092	1091	1089	1085	1079	1071	1062	1051	1038	1024
42	1092	1091	1088	1084	1078	1070	1061	1050	1037	1023
43	1091	1090	1087	1083	1077	1069	1060	1049	1036	1021
44	1089	1089	1086	1082	1076	1068	1058	1047	1034	1020
45	1088	1087	1085	1080	1074	1066	1057	1045	1032	1018

Inclination (variation from horizontal)

Zone 5W

Inclination (variation from horizontal)	Orientation (variation East or West from South)									
	0	**5**	**10**	**15**	**20**	**25**	**30**	**35**	**40**	**45**
0	803	803	803	803	803	803	803	803	803	803
1	809	809	809	809	809	809	808	808	808	807
2	816	816	816	816	816	815	814	814	813	812
3	823	823	823	823	822	821	820	819	818	817
4	830	830	830	829	828	827	826	825	823	822
5	837	837	836	835	835	833	832	830	828	826
6	843	843	842	842	841	839	838	836	833	831
7	849	849	849	848	846	845	843	841	838	835
8	855	855	855	854	852	850	848	846	843	839
9	861	861	860	859	858	856	853	850	847	843
10	867	867	866	865	863	861	858	855	851	847
11	873	872	872	870	868	866	863	859	856	851
12	878	878	877	875	873	871	868	864	860	855
13	883	883	882	880	878	875	872	868	863	858
14	888	888	887	885	883	880	876	872	867	862
15	893	893	892	890	887	884	880	876	871	865
16	898	898	896	894	892	888	884	880	874	868
17	902	902	901	899	896	892	888	883	877	871
18	907	906	905	903	900	896	892	886	880	874
19	911	910	909	907	904	900	895	890	883	876
20	915	914	913	910	907	903	898	893	886	879
21	918	918	916	914	911	907	901	895	889	881
22	922	921	920	917	914	910	904	898	891	883
23	925	925	923	921	917	913	907	901	893	885
24	928	928	926	923	920	915	910	903	896	887
25	931	931	929	926	923	918	912	905	897	889
26	934	933	932	929	925	920	914	907	899	890
27	936	936	934	931	927	922	916	909	901	892
28	939	938	936	933	929	924	918	910	902	893
29	941	940	938	935	931	926	919	912	903	894
30	943	942	940	937	933	927	921	913	904	895
31	944	944	942	939	934	929	922	914	905	895
32	946	945	943	940	936	930	923	915	906	896
33	947	946	944	941	937	931	924	916	906	896
34	948	947	945	942	937	932	924	916	907	896
35	949	948	946	943	938	932	925	916	907	896
36	949	949	947	943	938	932	925	916	907	896
37	950	949	947	943	939	933	925	916	906	895
38	950	949	947	944	939	932	925	916	906	895
39	950	949	947	943	939	932	925	916	905	894
40	949	949	947	943	938	932	924	915	904	893
41	949	948	946	942	937	931	923	914	903	892
42	948	948	945	942	937	930	922	913	902	890
43	947	947	944	941	936	929	921	912	901	889
44	946	945	943	940	934	928	920	910	899	887
45	945	944	942	938	933	926	918	908	897	885

Zone 5E

	Orientation (variation East or West from South)									
	0	**5**	**10**	**15**	**20**	**25**	**30**	**35**	**40**	**45**
0	820	820	820	820	820	820	820	820	820	820
1	827	827	826	826	826	826	826	825	825	824
2	834	834	834	833	833	832	832	831	830	830
3	841	841	841	840	840	839	838	837	836	835
4	848	848	848	847	846	845	844	843	841	839
5	855	855	854	854	853	851	850	848	846	844
6	861	861	861	860	859	857	856	854	851	849
7	868	868	867	866	865	863	861	859	856	853
8	874	874	873	872	871	869	867	864	861	857
9	880	880	879	878	877	874	872	869	865	862
10	886	886	885	884	882	880	877	874	870	866
11	892	892	891	889	888	885	882	878	874	870
12	898	897	896	895	893	890	887	883	878	873
13	903	903	902	900	898	895	891	887	882	877
14	908	908	907	905	903	899	896	891	886	880
15	913	913	912	910	907	904	900	895	890	884
16	918	918	916	915	912	908	904	899	893	887
17	923	922	921	919	916	912	908	903	897	890
18	927	927	925	923	920	916	912	906	900	893
19	931	931	930	927	924	920	915	909	903	896
20	935	935	933	931	928	924	918	912	906	898
21	939	939	937	935	931	927	922	915	908	900
22	943	942	941	938	935	930	925	918	911	903
23	946	946	944	941	938	933	927	921	913	905
24	949	949	947	944	941	936	930	923	915	907
25	952	952	950	947	943	939	932	925	917	908
26	955	955	953	950	946	941	935	927	919	910
27	958	957	955	952	948	943	937	929	921	911
28	960	959	958	955	950	945	939	931	922	912
29	962	962	960	957	952	947	940	932	923	914
30	964	964	962	959	954	948	942	934	924	914
31	966	965	963	960	956	950	943	935	925	915
32	967	967	965	961	957	951	944	936	926	915
33	969	968	966	963	958	952	945	936	927	916
34	970	969	967	964	959	953	945	937	927	916
35	971	970	968	964	959	953	946	937	927	916
36	971	970	968	965	960	954	946	937	927	915
37	972	971	969	965	960	954	946	937	927	915
38	972	971	969	965	960	954	946	937	926	914
39	972	971	969	965	960	954	945	936	926	913
40	971	971	968	965	960	953	945	935	925	912
41	971	970	968	964	959	952	944	934	923	911
42	970	969	967	963	958	951	943	933	922	910
43	969	968	966	962	957	950	942	932	921	908
44	968	967	965	961	956	949	940	930	919	906
45	967	966	964	960	954	947	939	929	917	905

Inclination (variation from horizontal)

Zone 6

Inclination (variation from horizontal)	Orientation (variation East or West from South)									
	0	**5**	**10**	**15**	**20**	**25**	**30**	**35**	**40**	**45**
0	789	789	789	789	789	789	789	789	789	789
1	796	796	796	795	795	795	795	794	794	794
2	803	803	802	802	802	801	801	800	799	799
3	810	809	809	809	808	808	807	806	805	803
4	816	816	816	815	815	814	812	811	810	808
5	823	823	822	822	821	819	818	816	815	813
6	829	829	828	828	827	825	824	822	819	817
7	835	835	835	834	832	831	829	827	824	821
8	841	841	841	840	838	836	834	832	829	825
9	847	847	846	845	844	842	839	836	833	830
10	853	853	852	851	849	847	844	841	837	833
11	859	858	857	856	854	852	849	845	842	837
12	864	864	863	861	859	857	853	850	846	841
13	869	869	868	866	864	861	858	854	849	844
14	874	874	873	871	869	866	862	858	853	848
15	879	879	878	876	873	870	866	862	857	851
16	884	883	882	880	878	874	870	866	860	854
17	888	888	887	885	882	878	874	869	863	857
18	892	892	891	889	886	882	878	872	866	860
19	897	896	895	893	890	886	881	876	869	862
20	901	900	899	896	893	889	884	879	872	865
21	904	904	902	900	897	893	887	881	875	867
22	908	907	906	903	900	896	890	884	877	869
23	911	911	909	907	903	899	893	887	880	872
24	914	914	912	910	906	901	896	889	882	873
25	917	917	915	912	909	904	898	891	884	875
26	920	919	918	915	911	906	900	893	885	877
27	922	922	920	917	913	908	902	895	887	878
28	925	924	922	920	916	910	904	897	888	879
29	927	926	925	922	917	912	906	898	890	880
30	929	928	926	923	919	914	907	900	891	881
31	931	930	928	925	921	915	908	901	892	882
32	932	931	930	926	922	916	910	902	892	882
33	933	933	931	928	923	917	910	902	893	883
34	935	934	932	929	924	918	911	903	893	883
35	935	935	933	929	925	919	912	903	894	883
36	936	935	933	930	925	919	912	903	894	883
37	937	936	934	930	926	919	912	903	893	882
38	937	936	934	931	926	919	912	903	893	882
39	937	936	934	931	926	919	912	903	892	881
40	937	936	934	930	925	919	911	902	892	880
41	936	936	933	930	925	918	911	901	891	879
42	936	935	933	929	924	918	910	900	890	878
43	935	934	932	928	923	917	909	899	888	876
44	934	933	931	927	922	915	907	898	887	875
45	933	932	930	926	921	914	906	896	885	873

Zone 7W

		Orientation (variation from south)								
		0	**5**	**10**	**15**	**20**	**25**	**30**	**35**	**40**	**45**
0	779	779	779	779	779	779	779	779	779	779
1	786	786	786	786	786	785	785	785	784	784
2	793	793	793	793	792	792	791	791	790	789
3	800	800	800	799	799	798	797	796	795	794
4	807	807	807	806	805	804	803	802	800	799
5	814	814	813	812	812	810	809	807	805	803
6	820	820	820	819	818	816	815	813	810	808
7	827	826	826	825	824	822	820	818	815	812
8	833	833	832	831	829	828	825	823	820	817
9	839	839	838	837	835	833	831	828	824	821
10	845	844	844	842	841	838	836	832	829	825
11	850	850	849	848	846	843	841	837	833	829
12	856	856	855	853	851	848	845	842	837	833
13	861	861	860	858	856	853	850	846	841	836
14	866	866	865	863	861	858	854	850	845	840
15	871	871	870	868	866	862	858	854	849	843
16	876	876	875	873	870	867	863	858	852	846
17	881	881	879	877	874	871	867	861	856	849
18	885	885	884	882	879	875	870	865	859	852
19	890	889	888	886	882	879	874	868	862	855
20	894	893	892	889	886	882	877	872	865	858
21	898	897	896	893	890	886	881	875	868	860
22	901	901	899	897	893	889	884	877	870	862
23	905	904	903	900	897	892	887	880	873	865
24	908	907	906	903	900	895	889	883	875	867
25	911	911	909	906	902	898	892	885	877	869
26	914	913	912	909	905	900	894	887	879	870
27	917	916	914	912	908	902	896	889	881	872
28	919	919	917	914	910	905	898	891	883	873
29	921	921	919	916	912	907	900	893	884	874
30	924	923	921	918	914	908	902	894	885	875
31	925	925	923	920	915	910	903	895	886	876
32	927	926	925	921	917	911	904	896	887	877
33	929	928	926	923	918	912	905	897	888	877
34	930	929	927	924	919	913	906	898	888	878
35	931	930	928	925	920	914	907	898	889	878
36	932	931	929	926	921	915	907	899	889	878
37	932	932	930	926	921	915	908	899	889	878
38	933	932	930	926	922	915	908	899	888	877
39	933	932	930	927	922	915	907	898	888	877
40	933	932	930	926	921	915	907	898	888	876
41	933	932	930	926	921	915	907	897	887	875
42	932	932	929	926	920	914	906	896	886	874
43	932	931	929	925	920	913	905	895	885	872
44	931	930	928	924	919	912	904	894	883	871
45	930	929	927	923	918	911	902	893	882	869

Inclination (variation from horizontal)

Zone 7E

		Orientation (variation East or West from South)								
		0	**5**	**10**	**15**	**20**	**25**	**30**	**35**	**40**	**45**
	0	735	735	735	735	735	735	735	735	735	735
	1	741	741	741	741	741	740	740	740	740	739
	2	747	747	747	747	746	746	746	745	744	744
	3	753	753	753	753	752	752	751	750	749	748
	4	759	759	759	759	758	757	756	755	753	752
	5	765	765	765	764	763	762	761	760	758	756
	6	771	771	770	770	769	767	766	764	762	760
	7	776	776	776	775	774	772	771	769	766	764
	8	782	782	781	780	779	777	775	773	771	768
	9	787	787	786	785	784	782	780	777	774	771
	10	792	792	791	790	789	787	784	781	778	775
	11	797	797	796	795	793	791	789	785	782	778
	12	802	802	801	800	798	795	793	789	786	781
	13	807	806	806	804	802	800	797	793	789	785
	14	811	811	810	808	806	804	800	797	792	787
	15	816	815	814	813	810	808	804	800	795	790
	16	820	819	818	817	814	811	808	803	798	793
	17	824	823	822	820	818	815	811	806	801	796
	18	827	827	826	824	821	818	814	809	804	798
	19	831	831	829	828	825	821	817	812	807	800
	20	835	834	833	831	828	824	820	815	809	803
	21	838	837	836	834	831	827	823	818	812	805
	22	841	841	839	837	834	830	825	820	814	807
	23	844	843	842	840	837	833	828	822	816	809
	24	847	846	845	842	839	835	830	824	818	810
	25	849	849	847	845	842	837	832	826	819	812
	26	852	851	850	847	844	839	834	828	821	813
	27	854	853	852	849	846	841	836	830	822	814
	28	856	855	854	851	848	843	837	831	823	815
	29	858	857	856	853	849	845	839	832	825	816
	30	859	859	857	855	851	846	840	833	825	817
	31	861	860	859	856	852	847	841	834	826	817
	32	862	862	860	857	853	848	842	835	827	818
	33	863	863	861	858	854	849	843	835	827	818
	34	864	864	862	859	855	850	843	836	827	818
	35	865	864	863	860	855	850	844	836	827	818
	36	865	865	863	860	856	850	844	836	827	818
	37	866	865	863	860	856	850	844	836	827	817
	38	866	865	863	860	856	850	844	836	827	817
	39	866	865	863	860	856	850	843	835	826	816
	40	866	865	863	860	855	850	843	835	825	815
	41	865	865	863	859	855	849	842	834	824	814
	42	865	864	862	859	854	848	841	833	823	813
	43	864	863	861	858	853	847	840	832	822	811
	44	863	862	860	857	852	846	839	830	821	810
	45	862	861	859	855	851	845	837	829	819	808

Inclination (variation from horizontal)

Zone 8S

				Orientation (variation East or West from South)						
	0	**5**	**10**	**15**	**20**	**25**	**30**	**35**	**40**	**45**
0	722	722	722	722	722	722	722	722	722	722
1	728	728	728	728	728	728	727	727	727	726
2	735	735	735	734	734	734	733	732	732	731
3	741	741	741	741	740	739	739	738	737	735
4	748	748	747	747	746	745	744	743	742	740
5	754	754	753	753	752	751	750	748	746	744
6	760	760	760	759	758	756	755	753	751	749
7	766	766	765	765	763	762	760	758	755	753
8	772	772	771	770	769	767	765	763	760	757
9	778	777	777	776	774	772	770	767	764	761
10	783	783	782	781	779	777	775	772	768	765
11	788	788	787	786	784	782	779	776	772	768
12	794	793	793	791	789	787	784	780	776	772
13	799	798	798	796	794	791	788	784	780	775
14	804	803	802	801	799	796	792	788	784	779
15	808	808	807	805	803	800	796	792	787	782
16	813	813	812	810	807	804	800	796	791	785
17	817	817	816	814	811	808	804	799	794	788
18	822	821	820	818	815	812	807	802	797	791
19	826	825	824	822	819	815	811	806	800	793
20	829	829	828	826	823	819	814	809	803	796
21	833	833	831	829	826	822	817	812	805	798
22	837	836	835	833	829	825	820	814	808	800
23	840	840	838	836	832	828	823	817	810	802
24	843	843	841	839	835	831	826	819	812	805
25	846	846	844	842	838	834	828	822	814	806
26	849	848	847	844	841	836	830	824	816	808
27	852	851	849	847	843	838	833	826	818	809
28	854	854	852	849	845	840	834	827	820	811
29	856	856	854	851	847	842	836	829	821	812
30	858	858	856	853	849	844	838	831	822	813
31	860	860	858	855	851	846	839	832	823	814
32	862	861	859	856	852	847	840	833	824	814
33	863	863	861	858	854	848	841	834	825	815
34	865	864	862	859	855	849	842	834	825	815
35	866	865	863	860	856	850	843	835	826	816
36	867	866	864	861	856	851	844	835	826	816
37	867	867	865	861	857	851	844	836	826	816
38	868	867	865	862	857	851	844	836	826	815
39	868	867	865	862	857	851	844	835	826	815
40	868	868	866	862	857	851	844	835	825	814
41	868	868	865	862	857	851	843	835	825	813
42	868	867	865	862	857	850	843	834	824	812
43	867	867	865	861	856	850	842	833	823	811
44	867	866	864	860	855	849	841	832	822	810
45	866	865	863	859	854	848	840	831	820	809

Inclination (variation from horizontal)

Zone 8E

Inclination (variation from horizontal)	Orientation (variation East or West from South)									
	0	**5**	**10**	**15**	**20**	**25**	**30**	**35**	**40**	**45**
0	731	731	731	731	731	731	731	731	731	731
1	737	737	737	737	737	737	736	736	736	735
2	744	744	744	744	743	743	742	742	741	740
3	751	751	750	750	750	749	748	747	746	745
4	757	757	757	756	756	755	754	752	751	749
5	764	763	763	762	762	760	759	758	756	754
6	770	770	769	768	767	766	764	763	760	758
7	776	776	775	774	773	771	770	767	765	762
8	782	782	781	780	779	777	775	772	769	766
9	788	787	787	786	784	782	780	777	774	770
10	793	793	792	791	789	787	784	781	778	774
11	799	798	798	796	794	792	789	786	782	778
12	804	804	803	801	799	797	794	790	786	782
13	809	809	808	806	804	801	798	794	790	785
14	814	814	813	811	809	806	802	798	794	788
15	819	818	817	816	813	810	806	802	797	792
16	823	823	822	820	818	814	810	806	801	795
17	828	827	826	824	822	818	814	809	804	798
18	832	832	831	829	826	822	818	813	807	801
19	836	836	835	833	830	826	821	816	810	803
20	840	840	838	836	833	829	825	819	813	806
21	844	844	842	840	837	833	828	822	815	808
22	848	847	846	843	840	836	831	825	818	811
23	851	851	849	847	843	839	834	828	820	813
24	854	854	852	850	846	842	836	830	823	815
25	857	857	855	853	849	844	839	832	825	817
26	860	860	858	855	852	847	841	834	827	818
27	863	862	861	858	854	849	843	836	828	820
28	865	865	863	860	856	851	845	838	830	821
29	868	867	865	862	858	853	847	840	831	822
30	870	869	867	864	860	855	849	841	833	823
31	872	871	869	866	862	857	850	842	834	824
32	873	873	871	868	863	858	851	844	835	825
33	875	874	872	869	865	859	852	844	835	825
34	876	875	873	870	866	860	853	845	836	826
35	877	876	875	871	867	861	854	846	836	826
36	878	877	875	872	868	862	855	846	837	826
37	879	878	876	873	868	862	855	846	837	826
38	879	879	877	873	868	862	855	846	837	826
39	880	879	877	873	869	862	855	846	836	825
40	880	879	877	873	869	862	855	846	836	825
41	880	879	877	873	868	862	854	845	835	824
42	879	879	877	873	868	862	854	845	834	823
43	879	878	876	872	867	861	853	844	833	822
44	878	878	875	872	867	860	852	843	832	820
45	877	877	874	871	866	859	851	842	831	819

Zone 9S

Inclination (variation from horizontal)	Orientation (variation East or West from South)									
	0	**5**	**10**	**15**	**20**	**25**	**30**	**35**	**40**	**45**
0	738	738	738	738	738	738	738	738	738	738
1	745	745	745	744	744	744	744	743	743	742
2	752	752	752	751	751	751	750	749	748	748
3	759	759	759	758	758	757	756	755	754	753
4	766	766	766	765	764	763	762	761	759	758
5	773	773	773	772	771	770	768	767	765	763
6	780	780	779	778	777	776	774	772	770	767
7	787	786	786	785	784	782	780	778	775	772
8	793	793	792	791	790	788	785	783	780	776
9	799	799	798	797	796	794	791	788	785	781
10	806	805	805	803	801	799	796	793	789	785
11	812	811	810	809	807	805	801	798	794	789
12	817	817	816	815	813	810	806	803	798	793
13	823	823	822	820	818	815	811	807	803	797
14	829	828	827	825	823	820	816	812	807	801
15	834	834	832	831	828	825	821	816	811	805
16	839	839	838	836	833	829	825	820	815	808
17	844	844	843	840	838	834	829	824	818	812
18	849	848	847	845	842	838	834	828	822	815
19	854	853	852	850	846	842	837	832	825	818
20	858	858	856	854	850	846	841	835	829	821
21	862	862	860	858	855	850	845	839	832	824
22	866	866	864	862	858	854	848	842	835	827
23	870	870	868	865	862	857	852	845	837	829
24	874	873	872	869	865	860	855	848	840	832
25	877	877	875	872	869	864	858	851	843	834
26	881	880	878	876	872	867	860	853	845	836
27	884	883	881	879	874	869	863	855	847	838
28	887	886	884	881	877	872	865	858	849	839
29	889	889	887	884	880	874	867	860	851	841
30	892	891	889	886	882	876	870	862	852	842
31	894	894	892	888	884	878	871	863	854	844
32	896	896	894	891	886	880	873	865	855	845
33	898	898	896	892	888	882	874	866	856	846
34	900	899	897	894	889	883	876	867	857	846
35	902	901	899	895	890	884	877	868	858	847
36	903	902	900	897	892	885	878	869	859	847
37	904	903	901	897	892	886	878	869	859	847
38	905	904	902	898	893	887	879	870	859	847
39	905	905	903	899	894	887	879	870	859	847
40	906	905	903	899	894	887	879	870	859	847
41	906	905	903	899	894	887	879	870	859	846
42	906	905	903	899	894	887	879	869	858	846
43	906	905	903	899	894	887	878	869	857	845
44	906	905	903	899	893	886	878	868	856	844
45	905	904	902	898	893	885	877	867	855	843

Zone 9E

	Orientation (variation East or West from South)									
	0	**5**	**10**	**15**	**20**	**25**	**30**	**35**	**40**	**45**
0	742	742	742	742	742	742	742	742	742	742
1	748	748	748	748	748	748	747	747	747	746
2	756	756	755	755	755	754	754	753	752	751
3	763	763	762	762	762	761	760	759	758	756
4	770	770	769	769	768	767	766	765	763	761
5	777	777	776	775	775	773	772	770	768	766
6	783	783	783	782	781	779	778	776	773	771
7	790	790	789	788	787	785	783	781	778	775
8	796	796	796	795	793	791	789	786	783	780
9	803	802	802	801	799	797	794	791	788	784
10	809	809	808	806	805	802	800	796	793	788
11	815	815	814	812	810	808	805	801	797	793
12	821	820	819	818	816	813	810	806	801	797
13	826	826	825	823	821	818	814	810	806	800
14	832	831	830	828	826	823	819	815	810	804
15	837	836	835	834	831	828	824	819	814	808
16	842	842	840	838	836	832	828	823	817	811
17	847	846	845	843	840	837	832	827	821	815
18	852	851	850	848	845	841	836	831	825	818
19	856	856	854	852	849	845	840	834	828	821
20	861	860	859	856	853	849	844	838	831	824
21	865	864	863	860	857	853	847	841	834	826
22	869	868	867	864	861	856	851	844	837	829
23	873	872	870	868	864	860	854	847	840	831
24	876	876	874	871	868	863	857	850	842	834
25	880	879	877	875	871	866	860	853	845	836
26	883	882	881	878	874	869	862	855	847	838
27	886	885	884	881	876	871	865	857	849	840
28	889	888	886	883	879	874	867	860	851	841
29	891	891	889	886	882	876	869	861	853	843
30	894	893	891	888	884	878	871	863	854	844
31	896	895	894	890	886	880	873	865	855	845
32	898	898	896	892	888	882	875	866	857	846
33	900	899	897	894	889	883	876	867	858	847
34	902	901	899	895	891	884	877	868	858	847
35	903	902	900	897	892	886	878	869	859	848
36	904	904	901	898	893	887	879	870	860	848
37	905	905	902	899	894	887	880	870	860	848
38	906	905	903	900	894	888	880	871	860	848
39	907	906	904	900	895	888	880	871	860	848
40	907	906	904	900	895	888	880	871	860	848
41	907	907	904	900	895	888	880	870	859	847
42	907	907	904	900	895	888	880	870	859	846
43	907	906	904	900	895	888	879	869	858	845
44	907	906	903	900	894	887	878	868	857	844
45	906	905	903	899	893	886	877	867	856	843

Inclination (variation from horizontal)

Zone 10

Inclination (variation from horizontal)	Orientation (variation East or West from South)									
	0	5	10	15	20	25	30	35	40	45
0	750	750	750	750	750	750	750	750	750	750
1	757	757	757	757	757	757	756	756	756	755
2	765	765	764	764	764	763	763	762	761	760
3	772	772	772	771	771	770	769	768	767	765
4	779	779	779	778	777	776	775	774	772	770
5	786	786	785	785	784	783	781	779	777	775
6	793	793	792	791	790	789	787	785	783	780
7	799	799	799	798	796	795	793	790	788	785
8	806	806	805	804	803	801	798	796	793	789
9	812	812	811	810	808	806	804	801	797	794
10	818	818	817	816	814	812	809	806	802	798
11	825	824	823	822	820	817	814	811	807	802
12	830	830	829	828	825	823	819	815	811	806
13	836	836	835	833	831	828	824	820	815	810
14	842	841	840	838	836	833	829	824	819	814
15	847	847	845	843	841	838	833	829	823	817
16	852	852	850	848	846	842	838	833	827	821
17	857	857	855	853	850	847	842	837	831	824
18	862	861	860	858	855	851	846	841	834	827
19	866	866	865	862	859	855	850	844	838	831
20	871	870	869	867	863	859	854	848	841	833
21	875	875	873	871	867	863	857	851	844	836
22	879	879	877	874	871	866	861	854	847	839
23	883	882	881	878	874	870	864	857	850	841
24	887	886	884	882	878	873	867	860	852	844
25	890	890	888	885	881	876	870	863	855	846
26	893	893	891	888	884	879	873	865	857	848
27	896	896	894	891	887	882	875	868	859	850
28	899	899	897	894	890	884	877	870	861	851
29	902	901	899	896	892	886	880	872	863	853
30	904	904	902	899	894	888	882	873	864	854
31	907	906	904	901	896	890	883	875	866	855
32	909	908	906	903	898	892	885	876	867	856
33	911	910	908	904	900	894	886	878	868	857
34	912	912	909	906	901	895	887	879	869	858
35	914	913	911	907	902	896	888	879	869	858
36	915	914	912	908	903	897	889	880	870	858
37	916	915	913	909	904	898	890	881	870	858
38	917	916	914	910	905	898	890	881	870	858
39	917	917	914	911	905	899	890	881	870	858
40	918	917	915	911	906	899	890	881	870	858
41	918	917	915	911	906	899	890	880	869	857
42	918	917	915	911	905	898	890	880	869	856
43	918	917	914	910	905	898	889	879	868	855
44	917	916	914	910	904	897	889	878	867	854
45	916	916	913	909	904	896	888	877	866	853

Zone 11

Inclination (variation from horizontal)	Orientation (variation East or West from South)									
	0	**5**	**10**	**15**	**20**	**25**	**30**	**35**	**40**	**45**
0	750	750	750	750	750	750	750	750	750	750
1	756	756	756	756	756	755	755	755	754	754
2	763	763	763	762	762	762	761	760	760	759
3	769	769	769	769	768	767	767	766	765	763
4	776	776	775	775	774	773	772	771	769	768
5	782	782	782	781	780	779	778	776	774	772
6	788	788	788	787	786	785	783	781	779	777
7	794	794	794	793	791	790	788	786	783	781
8	800	800	799	798	797	795	793	791	788	785
9	806	806	805	804	802	800	798	795	792	789
10	811	811	810	809	807	805	803	800	796	792
11	817	816	816	814	812	810	807	804	800	796
12	822	822	821	819	817	815	812	808	804	800
13	827	827	826	824	822	819	816	812	808	803
14	832	831	830	829	827	824	820	816	811	806
15	837	836	835	833	831	828	824	820	815	809
16	841	841	840	838	835	832	828	823	818	812
17	845	845	844	842	839	836	832	827	821	815
18	849	849	848	846	843	840	835	830	824	818
19	853	853	852	850	847	843	838	833	827	820
20	857	857	856	853	850	846	842	836	830	823
21	861	860	859	857	854	850	845	839	832	825
22	864	864	862	860	857	853	848	841	835	827
23	868	867	866	863	860	855	850	844	837	829
24	871	870	869	866	863	858	853	846	839	831
25	874	873	871	869	865	861	855	848	841	833
26	876	876	874	871	868	863	857	850	843	834
27	879	878	877	874	870	865	859	852	844	835
28	881	881	879	876	872	867	861	854	846	837
29	883	883	881	878	874	869	863	855	847	838
30	885	884	883	880	876	870	864	857	848	838
31	887	886	884	881	877	872	865	858	849	839
32	888	888	886	883	879	873	866	859	850	840
33	890	889	887	884	880	874	867	859	850	840
34	891	890	888	885	881	875	868	860	851	840
35	892	891	889	886	881	876	868	860	851	840
36	892	892	890	887	882	876	869	860	851	840
37	893	892	890	887	882	876	869	860	851	840
38	893	893	891	887	882	876	869	860	850	839
39	893	893	891	887	882	876	869	860	850	839
40	893	893	891	887	882	876	868	859	849	838
41	893	892	890	887	882	875	868	859	848	837
42	893	892	890	886	881	875	867	858	847	836
43	892	891	889	885	880	874	866	857	846	834
44	891	890	888	884	879	873	865	855	845	833
45	890	889	887	883	878	872	863	854	843	831

Zone 12

		Orientation (variation East or West from South)								
		0	**5**	**10**	**15**	**20**	**25**	**30**	**35**	**40**	**45**
0		805	805	805	805	805	805	805	805	805	805
1		812	812	811	811	811	811	811	810	810	809
2		819	819	819	818	818	817	817	816	815	814
3		826	826	826	825	825	824	823	822	821	820
4		833	833	833	832	831	830	829	828	826	824
5		840	840	839	839	838	837	835	833	831	829
6		847	847	846	845	844	843	841	839	837	834
7		853	853	853	852	850	849	847	844	842	839
8		860	860	859	858	856	854	852	849	846	843
9		866	866	865	864	862	860	857	854	851	847
10		872	872	871	870	868	865	863	859	856	851
11		878	878	877	875	873	871	868	864	860	855
12		884	883	882	881	879	876	873	869	864	859
13		889	889	888	886	884	881	877	873	868	863
14		894	894	893	891	889	886	882	877	872	867
15		900	899	898	896	894	890	886	881	876	870
16		905	904	903	901	898	895	890	885	880	873
17		909	909	908	906	903	899	894	889	883	877
18		914	913	912	910	907	903	898	893	887	880
19		918	918	916	914	911	907	902	896	890	882
20		922	922	921	918	915	911	906	900	893	885
21		926	926	924	922	919	914	909	903	896	888
22		930	930	928	926	922	918	912	906	898	890
23		934	933	932	929	925	921	915	908	901	892
24		937	937	935	932	928	924	918	911	903	894
25		940	940	938	935	931	926	920	913	905	896
26		943	943	941	938	934	929	923	915	907	898
27		946	945	944	941	937	931	925	917	909	899
28		949	948	946	943	939	934	927	919	911	901
29		951	950	948	945	941	935	929	921	912	902
30		953	952	951	947	943	937	930	922	913	903
31		955	954	952	949	945	939	932	924	914	904
32		957	956	954	951	946	940	933	925	915	905
33		958	958	955	952	947	941	934	926	916	905
34		959	959	957	953	948	942	935	926	916	905
35		961	960	958	954	949	943	936	927	917	905
36		961	961	959	955	950	944	936	927	917	905
37		962	961	959	956	950	944	936	927	917	905
38		962	962	959	956	951	944	936	927	916	905
39		963	962	960	956	951	944	936	927	916	904
40		962	962	959	956	951	944	936	926	915	903
41		962	961	959	955	950	943	935	925	914	902
42		962	961	959	955	949	943	934	925	913	901
43		961	960	958	954	949	942	933	923	912	899
44		960	959	957	953	948	941	932	922	911	898
45		959	958	956	952	946	939	931	921	909	896

Inclination (variation from horizontal)

Zone 13

Inclination (variation from horizontal) \ Orientation (variation East or West from South)	0	5	10	15	20	25	30	35	40	45
0	789	789	789	789	789	789	789	789	789	789
1	795	795	795	795	795	795	794	794	794	793
2	802	802	802	802	801	801	800	800	799	798
3	809	808	808	808	807	807	806	805	804	803
4	815	815	814	814	813	812	811	810	809	807
5	821	821	821	820	819	818	817	815	813	811
6	827	827	826	826	825	823	822	820	818	815
7	833	833	832	831	830	829	827	825	822	819
8	839	838	838	837	835	834	832	829	826	823
9	844	844	843	842	841	839	836	834	831	827
10	849	849	848	847	846	844	841	838	835	831
11	855	854	853	852	850	848	845	842	838	834
12	859	859	858	857	855	853	850	846	842	838
13	864	864	863	862	860	857	854	850	846	841
14	869	869	868	866	864	861	858	854	849	844
15	873	873	872	870	868	865	861	857	852	847
16	878	877	876	874	872	869	865	861	855	850
17	882	881	880	878	876	872	869	864	858	852
18	886	885	884	882	879	876	872	867	861	855
19	889	889	888	886	883	879	875	870	864	857
20	893	892	891	889	886	882	878	873	866	860
21	896	896	894	892	889	885	881	875	869	862
22	899	899	898	895	892	888	883	878	871	863
23	902	902	900	898	895	891	886	880	873	865
24	905	905	903	901	897	893	888	882	875	867
25	908	907	906	903	900	895	890	884	876	868
26	910	909	908	905	902	897	892	885	878	870
27	912	912	910	907	904	899	894	887	879	871
28	914	914	912	909	906	901	895	888	880	872
29	916	915	914	911	907	902	896	889	881	872
30	917	917	915	912	909	904	898	890	882	873
31	919	918	916	914	910	905	898	891	883	874
32	920	919	918	915	911	906	899	892	883	874
33	921	920	918	915	911	906	900	892	884	874
34	921	921	919	916	912	907	900	893	884	874
35	922	921	920	917	912	907	900	892	884	874
36	922	922	920	917	913	907	900	892	883	873
37	922	922	920	917	913	907	900	892	883	873
38	922	922	920	917	912	907	900	892	882	872
39	922	921	919	916	912	906	899	891	881	871
40	921	921	919	916	911	905	898	890	880	870
41	921	920	918	915	910	905	897	889	879	868
42	920	919	917	914	909	903	896	888	878	867
43	919	918	916	913	908	902	895	886	876	865
44	917	916	915	911	907	901	893	885	875	863
45	916	915	913	910	905	899	891	883	873	861

Zone 14

	Orientation (variation East or West from South)									
	0	**5**	**10**	**15**	**20**	**25**	**30**	**35**	**40**	**45**
0	701	701	701	701	701	701	701	701	701	701
1	707	706	706	706	706	706	706	705	705	705
2	713	713	712	712	712	711	711	710	710	709
3	719	719	718	718	718	717	716	715	714	713
4	725	725	724	724	723	722	721	720	719	717
5	730	730	730	729	729	728	726	725	723	722
6	736	736	736	735	734	733	731	730	728	725
7	742	741	741	740	739	738	736	734	732	729
8	747	747	746	745	744	743	741	738	736	733
9	752	752	752	751	749	747	745	743	740	737
10	758	757	757	755	754	752	750	747	744	740
11	762	762	761	760	759	756	754	751	747	744
12	767	767	766	765	763	761	758	755	751	747
13	772	772	771	769	768	765	762	759	755	750
14	776	776	775	774	772	769	766	762	758	753
15	781	781	780	778	776	773	770	766	761	756
16	785	785	784	782	780	777	773	769	764	759
17	789	789	788	786	784	780	777	772	767	762
18	793	793	792	790	787	784	780	775	770	764
19	797	796	795	793	791	787	783	778	773	767
20	800	800	799	797	794	790	786	781	775	769
21	804	803	802	800	797	793	789	784	778	771
22	807	806	805	803	800	796	792	786	780	773
23	810	809	808	806	803	799	794	789	782	775
24	813	812	811	809	806	802	797	791	784	777
25	815	815	814	811	808	804	799	793	786	779
26	818	818	816	814	810	806	801	795	788	780
27	820	820	818	816	813	808	803	797	790	782
28	823	822	821	818	815	810	805	798	791	783
29	825	824	822	820	816	812	806	800	792	784
30	826	826	824	822	818	813	808	801	793	785
31	828	827	826	823	819	815	809	802	794	785
32	829	829	827	825	821	816	810	803	795	786
33	831	830	828	826	822	817	811	804	796	787
34	832	831	830	827	823	818	812	804	796	787
35	833	832	830	828	824	818	812	805	796	787
36	833	833	831	828	824	819	812	805	796	787
37	834	833	832	829	824	819	813	805	796	787
38	834	834	832	829	825	819	813	805	796	786
39	835	834	832	829	825	819	813	805	796	786
40	835	834	832	829	825	819	812	804	795	785
41	834	834	832	829	824	819	812	804	795	784
42	834	833	831	828	824	818	811	803	794	783
43	833	833	831	828	823	817	810	802	793	782
44	833	832	830	827	822	816	809	801	792	781
45	832	831	829	826	821	815	808	800	790	779

Inclination (variation from horizontal)

Zone 15

Inclination (variation from horizontal)	Orientation (variation East or West from South)									
	0	**5**	**10**	**15**	**20**	**25**	**30**	**35**	**40**	**45**
0	758	758	758	758	758	758	758	758	758	758
1	766	765	765	765	765	765	764	764	764	763
2	773	773	773	773	772	772	771	771	770	769
3	781	781	781	780	780	779	778	777	776	774
4	789	789	788	788	787	786	785	783	781	779
5	796	796	796	795	794	793	791	789	787	785
6	804	803	803	802	801	799	797	795	793	790
7	811	811	810	809	808	806	804	801	798	795
8	818	818	817	816	814	812	810	807	804	800
9	825	824	824	822	821	818	816	812	809	805
10	831	831	830	829	827	824	821	818	814	809
11	838	838	837	835	833	830	827	823	819	814
12	844	844	843	841	839	836	833	828	824	818
13	851	850	849	847	845	842	838	833	828	823
14	857	856	855	853	850	847	843	838	833	827
15	862	862	861	859	856	852	848	843	837	831
16	868	868	866	864	861	858	853	848	842	835
17	874	873	872	869	866	862	858	852	846	839
18	879	878	877	875	871	867	862	856	850	842
19	884	883	882	880	876	872	867	861	854	846
20	889	888	887	884	881	876	871	865	857	849
21	893	893	891	889	885	880	875	868	861	852
22	898	897	896	893	889	884	879	872	864	855
23	902	902	900	897	893	888	882	875	867	858
24	906	906	904	901	897	892	886	879	870	861
25	910	910	908	905	901	896	889	882	873	863
26	914	913	912	909	904	899	892	884	876	866
27	918	917	915	912	908	902	895	887	878	868
28	921	920	918	915	911	905	898	890	880	870
29	924	923	921	918	913	908	900	892	883	872
30	927	926	924	921	916	910	903	894	885	874
31	930	929	927	923	918	912	905	896	886	875
32	932	931	929	926	921	914	907	898	888	876
33	934	933	931	928	923	916	909	900	889	878
34	936	935	933	930	925	918	910	901	890	879
35	938	937	935	931	926	920	912	902	891	879
36	940	939	936	933	928	921	913	903	892	880
37	941	940	938	934	929	922	914	904	893	880
38	942	941	939	935	930	923	914	904	893	881
39	943	942	940	936	930	923	915	905	893	881
40	944	943	940	936	931	924	915	905	894	881
41	944	943	941	937	931	924	915	905	893	880
42	944	944	941	937	931	924	915	905	893	880
43	944	944	941	937	931	924	915	904	892	879
44	944	943	941	937	931	923	914	904	892	878
45	944	943	940	936	930	923	914	903	891	877

Zone 16

Inclination (variation from horizontal)	Orientation (variation East or West from South)									
	0	**5**	**10**	**15**	**20**	**25**	**30**	**35**	**40**	**45**
0	712	712	712	712	712	712	712	712	712	712
1	718	718	718	718	718	718	717	717	717	716
2	725	725	725	725	725	724	724	723	722	721
3	732	732	732	732	731	730	730	729	727	726
4	739	739	739	738	737	737	735	734	733	731
5	746	746	745	745	744	743	741	740	738	736
6	752	752	752	751	750	749	747	745	743	740
7	759	759	758	757	756	754	753	750	748	745
8	765	765	764	763	762	760	758	755	753	749
9	771	771	771	769	768	766	763	761	757	754
10	777	777	776	775	773	771	769	765	762	758
11	783	783	782	781	779	777	774	770	766	762
12	789	789	788	786	784	782	779	775	771	766
13	795	794	793	792	789	787	783	779	775	770
14	800	800	799	797	795	792	788	784	779	774
15	805	805	804	802	799	796	792	788	783	777
16	810	810	809	807	804	801	797	792	787	781
17	815	815	814	812	809	805	801	796	791	784
18	820	819	818	816	813	810	805	800	794	788
19	824	824	823	820	818	814	809	804	798	791
20	829	828	827	825	822	818	813	807	801	794
21	833	833	831	829	826	821	816	811	804	797
22	837	837	835	833	829	825	820	814	807	799
23	841	840	839	836	833	828	823	817	810	802
24	844	844	842	840	836	832	826	820	812	804
25	848	847	846	843	839	835	829	822	815	806
26	851	851	849	846	843	838	832	825	817	808
27	854	854	852	849	845	840	834	827	819	810
28	857	857	855	852	848	843	837	830	821	812
29	860	859	858	855	851	845	839	832	823	814
30	862	862	860	857	853	848	841	834	825	815
31	865	864	862	859	855	850	843	835	826	817
32	867	866	864	861	857	851	845	837	828	818
33	869	868	866	863	859	853	846	838	829	819
34	871	870	868	865	860	854	847	839	830	820
35	872	871	869	866	862	856	849	840	831	820
36	873	873	871	867	863	857	850	841	831	821
37	875	874	872	868	864	858	850	842	832	821
38	876	875	873	869	865	858	851	842	832	821
39	876	876	873	870	865	859	851	842	832	821
40	877	876	874	870	866	859	851	843	832	821
41	877	876	874	871	866	859	852	842	832	821
42	877	877	874	871	866	859	851	842	832	820
43	877	877	874	871	866	859	851	842	831	819
44	877	876	874	870	865	859	850	841	830	818
45	877	876	874	870	865	858	850	840	829	817

Zone 17

Inclination (variation from horizontal)	Orientation (variation East or West from South)									
	0	**5**	**10**	**15**	**20**	**25**	**30**	**35**	**40**	**45**
0	691	691	691	691	691	691	691	691	691	691
1	697	697	697	697	697	697	696	696	696	695
2	704	703	703	703	703	702	702	701	700	700
3	710	710	710	709	709	708	707	706	705	704
4	716	716	716	715	714	714	713	711	710	708
5	722	722	722	721	720	719	718	716	715	713
6	728	728	727	727	726	724	723	721	719	717
7	734	734	733	732	731	730	728	726	724	721
8	740	739	739	738	737	735	733	731	728	725
9	745	745	744	743	742	740	738	735	732	729
10	750	750	750	748	747	745	742	739	736	733
11	756	756	755	753	752	750	747	744	740	736
12	761	761	760	758	757	754	751	748	744	740
13	766	766	765	763	761	759	756	752	748	743
14	771	770	769	768	766	763	760	756	751	747
15	775	775	774	772	770	767	764	760	755	750
16	780	780	779	777	774	771	768	763	758	753
17	784	784	783	781	778	775	771	767	762	756
18	788	788	787	785	782	779	775	770	765	759
19	792	792	791	789	786	783	778	773	768	761
20	796	796	795	793	790	786	782	776	771	764
21	800	800	798	796	793	789	785	779	773	766
22	804	803	802	800	797	792	788	782	776	769
23	807	806	805	803	800	795	791	785	778	771
24	810	810	808	806	803	798	793	787	781	773
25	813	813	811	809	805	801	796	790	783	775
26	816	815	814	811	808	804	798	792	785	777
27	819	818	816	814	810	806	800	794	786	778
28	821	821	819	816	813	808	802	796	788	780
29	823	823	821	819	815	810	804	797	790	781
30	826	825	823	821	817	812	806	799	791	782
31	827	827	825	822	818	813	807	800	792	783
32	829	829	827	824	820	815	809	801	793	784
33	831	830	828	826	821	816	810	803	794	785
34	832	832	830	827	823	817	811	803	795	785
35	833	833	831	828	824	818	812	804	795	785
36	834	834	832	829	825	819	812	805	796	786
37	835	835	833	830	825	820	813	805	796	786
38	836	835	833	830	826	820	813	805	796	786
39	836	836	834	831	826	820	813	805	796	785
40	837	836	834	831	826	820	813	805	796	785
41	837	836	834	831	826	820	813	805	795	784
42	837	836	834	831	826	820	813	804	795	784
43	836	836	834	830	826	820	812	804	794	783
44	836	835	833	830	825	819	811	803	793	782
45	835	835	832	829	824	818	811	802	792	780

Zone 18

					Orientation (variation East or West from South)						
		0	**5**	**10**	**15**	**20**	**25**	**30**	**35**	**40**	**45**
	0	645	645	645	645	645	645	645	645	645	645
	1	650	650	650	650	650	649	649	649	649	648
	2	656	656	655	655	655	655	654	654	653	652
	3	661	661	661	661	660	660	659	658	657	656
	4	667	667	666	666	665	664	664	663	661	660
	5	672	672	671	671	670	669	668	667	665	664
	6	677	677	677	676	675	674	673	671	669	667
	7	682	682	682	681	680	679	677	675	673	671
	8	687	687	687	686	685	683	681	679	677	675
	9	692	692	691	691	689	688	686	683	681	678
	10	697	697	696	695	694	692	690	687	684	681
	11	701	701	701	699	698	696	694	691	688	684
	12	706	706	705	704	702	700	698	695	691	687
	13	710	710	709	708	706	704	701	698	695	691
	14	714	714	713	712	710	708	705	702	698	693
	15	718	718	717	716	714	711	708	705	701	696
	16	722	722	721	720	718	715	712	708	704	699
	17	726	726	725	723	721	718	715	711	706	701
	18	730	729	728	727	724	721	718	714	709	704
	19	733	733	732	730	728	725	721	717	712	706
	20	736	736	735	733	731	728	724	719	714	709
	21	740	739	738	736	734	730	726	722	717	711
	22	742	742	741	739	736	733	729	724	719	713
	23	745	745	744	742	739	736	731	726	721	714
	24	748	748	746	744	742	738	734	729	723	716
	25	751	750	749	747	744	740	736	730	724	718
	26	753	752	751	749	746	742	738	732	726	719
	27	755	755	753	751	748	744	739	734	728	720
	28	757	757	755	753	750	746	741	735	729	722
	29	759	758	757	755	752	748	743	737	730	723
	30	761	760	759	756	753	749	744	738	731	724
	31	762	762	760	758	755	750	745	739	732	724
	32	764	763	762	759	756	751	746	740	733	725
	33	765	764	763	760	757	752	747	741	734	726
	34	766	765	764	761	758	753	748	741	734	726
	35	767	766	765	762	758	754	748	742	734	726
	36	767	767	765	763	759	754	749	742	735	726
	37	768	767	766	763	759	755	749	742	735	726
	38	768	768	766	763	760	755	749	742	735	726
	39	768	768	766	764	760	755	749	742	734	725
	40	768	768	766	763	760	755	749	742	734	725
	41	768	768	766	763	759	754	748	741	733	724
	42	768	767	766	763	759	754	748	741	733	723
	43	767	767	765	762	758	753	747	740	732	722
	44	767	766	764	762	758	752	746	739	731	721
	45	766	765	763	761	757	751	745	738	729	720

Inclination (variation from horizontal)

Zone 19

						Orientation (variation East or West from South)					
		0	**5**	**10**	**15**	**20**	**25**	**30**	**35**	**40**	**45**
	0	617	617	617	617	617	617	617	617	617	617
	1	622	622	621	621	621	621	621	621	620	620
	2	627	627	627	627	626	626	625	625	624	624
	3	632	632	632	632	631	631	630	629	628	627
	4	637	637	637	637	636	635	635	634	632	631
	5	642	642	642	642	641	640	639	638	636	635
	6	647	647	647	646	646	645	643	642	640	638
	7	652	652	652	651	650	649	647	646	644	642
	8	657	657	656	656	655	653	652	650	647	645
	9	662	662	661	660	659	657	655	653	651	648
	10	666	666	665	664	663	661	659	657	654	651
	11	671	670	670	669	667	665	663	661	658	654
	12	675	675	674	673	671	669	667	664	661	657
	13	679	679	678	677	675	673	670	667	664	660
	14	683	683	682	681	679	677	674	671	667	663
	15	687	686	686	684	682	680	677	674	670	666
Inclination (variation from horizontal)	**16**	690	690	689	688	686	683	680	677	673	668
	17	694	694	693	691	689	687	683	680	675	671
	18	697	697	696	695	692	690	686	682	678	673
	19	701	700	699	698	696	693	689	685	680	675
	20	704	703	702	701	698	695	692	687	683	677
	21	707	706	705	704	701	698	694	690	685	679
	22	710	709	708	706	704	701	697	692	687	681
	23	712	712	711	709	706	703	699	694	689	683
	24	715	715	713	711	709	705	701	696	691	684
	25	717	717	716	714	711	707	703	698	692	686
	26	720	719	718	716	713	709	705	700	694	687
	27	722	721	720	718	715	711	707	701	695	689
	28	724	723	722	720	717	713	708	703	697	690
	29	725	725	724	721	718	714	710	704	698	691
	30	727	727	725	723	720	716	711	705	699	692
	31	729	728	727	724	721	717	712	706	700	692
	32	730	729	728	726	722	718	713	707	700	693
	33	731	730	729	727	723	719	714	708	701	693
	34	732	731	730	728	724	720	715	709	702	694
	35	733	732	731	728	725	721	715	709	702	694
	36	733	733	731	729	725	721	716	709	702	694
	37	734	733	732	729	726	721	716	709	702	694
	38	734	734	732	730	726	722	716	709	702	694
	39	735	734	732	730	726	722	716	709	702	693
	40	735	734	732	730	726	721	716	709	701	693
	41	734	734	732	730	726	721	715	708	701	692
	42	734	734	732	729	725	721	715	708	700	691
	43	734	733	731	729	725	720	714	707	699	690
	44	733	732	731	728	724	719	713	706	698	689
	45	732	732	730	727	723	718	712	705	697	688

Zone 20

| | | \multicolumn{10}{c}{Orientation (variation East or West from South)} | | | | | | | | |
		0	5	10	15	20	25	30	35	40	45
\multirow{46}{*}{Inclination (variation from horizontal)}	0	599	599	599	599	599	599	599	599	599	599
	1	604	604	603	603	603	603	603	603	602	602
	2	609	609	609	608	608	608	607	607	606	606
	3	614	614	614	613	613	612	612	611	610	609
	4	619	619	619	618	618	617	616	615	614	613
	5	624	624	623	623	622	621	620	619	618	616
	6	629	629	628	628	627	626	625	623	622	620
	7	633	633	633	632	631	630	629	627	625	623
	8	638	638	637	637	636	634	633	631	629	626
	9	642	642	642	641	640	638	637	634	632	630
	10	647	647	646	645	644	642	640	638	635	633
	11	651	651	650	649	648	646	644	642	639	636
	12	655	655	654	653	652	650	648	645	642	638
	13	659	659	658	657	656	654	651	648	645	641
	14	663	663	662	661	659	657	654	651	648	644
	15	667	667	666	665	663	661	658	655	651	647
	16	671	670	669	668	666	664	661	657	654	649
	17	674	674	673	672	670	667	664	660	656	652
	18	677	677	676	675	673	670	667	663	659	654
	19	681	680	679	678	676	673	670	666	661	656
	20	684	683	682	681	679	676	672	668	663	658
	21	687	686	685	684	681	678	675	670	666	660
	22	689	689	688	686	684	681	677	673	668	662
	23	692	692	691	689	686	683	679	675	670	664
	24	695	694	693	691	689	685	681	677	671	665
	25	697	697	695	694	691	688	683	679	673	667
	26	699	699	698	696	693	689	685	680	675	668
	27	701	701	700	698	695	691	687	682	676	670
	28	703	703	701	699	697	693	689	683	677	671
	29	705	704	703	701	698	694	690	685	678	672
	30	706	706	705	703	700	696	691	686	680	673
	31	708	708	706	704	701	697	692	687	680	673
	32	709	709	707	705	702	698	693	688	681	674
	33	710	710	709	706	703	699	694	688	682	675
	34	711	711	710	707	704	700	695	689	682	675
	35	712	712	710	708	705	701	696	690	683	675
	36	713	712	711	709	705	701	696	690	683	675
	37	713	713	711	709	706	701	696	690	683	675
	38	714	713	712	709	706	702	696	690	683	675
	39	714	714	712	710	706	702	696	690	683	675
	40	714	714	712	710	706	702	696	690	682	674
	41	714	713	712	709	706	701	696	689	682	674
	42	714	713	712	709	706	701	695	689	681	673
	43	713	713	711	709	705	700	695	688	681	672
	44	713	712	711	708	704	700	694	687	680	671
	45	712	711	710	707	703	699	693	686	679	670

Zone 21

Inclination (variation from horizontal)	Orientation (variation East or West from South)									
	0	**5**	**10**	**15**	**20**	**25**	**30**	**35**	**40**	**45**
0	711	711	711	711	711	711	711	711	711	711
1	717	717	717	716	716	716	716	715	715	715
2	723	723	723	722	722	722	721	721	720	719
3	729	729	729	728	728	727	727	726	725	723
4	735	735	735	734	734	733	732	731	729	728
5	741	741	741	740	739	738	737	735	734	732
6	747	747	746	746	745	743	742	740	738	736
7	752	752	752	751	750	748	747	745	742	740
8	758	758	757	756	755	753	751	749	746	743
9	763	763	762	761	760	758	756	753	750	747
10	768	768	768	766	765	763	760	758	754	751
11	774	773	773	771	770	767	765	762	758	754
12	778	778	777	776	774	772	769	766	762	758
13	783	783	782	781	779	776	773	769	765	761
14	788	787	787	785	783	780	777	773	769	764
15	792	792	791	789	787	784	781	777	772	767
16	797	796	795	793	791	788	784	780	775	770
17	801	800	799	797	795	792	788	783	778	772
18	805	804	803	801	798	795	791	786	781	775
19	808	808	807	805	802	799	794	789	784	777
20	812	812	810	808	805	802	797	792	786	780
21	815	815	814	811	809	805	800	795	789	782
22	819	818	817	815	812	808	803	797	791	784
23	822	821	820	818	814	810	805	800	793	786
24	825	824	823	820	817	813	808	802	795	788
25	827	827	825	823	820	815	810	804	797	789
26	830	829	828	825	822	817	812	806	799	790
27	832	832	830	828	824	819	814	807	800	792
28	835	834	832	830	826	821	816	809	801	793
29	837	836	834	832	828	823	817	810	803	794
30	838	838	836	833	830	825	819	812	804	795
31	840	839	838	835	831	826	820	813	804	795
32	841	841	839	836	832	827	821	814	805	796
33	843	842	840	837	833	828	822	814	806	796
34	844	843	841	838	834	829	822	815	806	797
35	845	844	842	839	835	830	823	815	806	797
36	846	845	843	840	836	830	823	816	807	797
37	846	845	844	840	836	830	824	816	806	796
38	846	846	844	841	836	830	824	815	806	796
39	847	846	844	841	836	830	823	815	806	795
40	847	846	844	841	836	830	823	815	805	795
41	846	846	844	840	836	830	823	814	804	794
42	846	845	843	840	835	829	822	813	803	793
43	845	845	843	839	834	828	821	812	802	791
44	845	844	842	838	834	827	820	811	801	790
45	844	843	841	837	832	826	819	810	800	788

The last factor in the equation is an estimation of the shading that could affect the PV system. The shade factor takes into account objects which are further than 10m away from the centre midpoint of the array and objects which are at or less than 10m away from the centre midpoint of the array. Objects that fall into these brackets use different procedures to calculate the de-rating factor applied to the system performance calculation.

Objects further than 10m away from the centre midpoint of the array

Where it is obvious that there is no object creating any form of shading on the array, the SF can be omitted and a value of 1 can be used in the calculation.

Where the installer suspects that shading may occur, a sun path chart should be completed outlining the horizon line using the following procedure:

Standing as near to the base and centre of the proposed array site and facing due south, draw a line showing the edge of any object which are visible on the horizon. This is deemed the horizontal line.

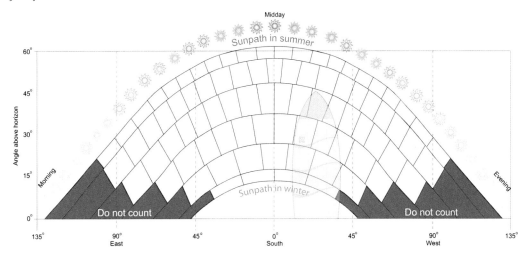

From the MCS guide to installation of PV systems

The horizontal line shown in the example above indicates a tall building on the horizon of the proposed array.

After this horizontal line has been drawn on the diagram, the number of segments that are either touched by or fall under the line shall be counted. The example in the previous image has 11 segments which are either touched

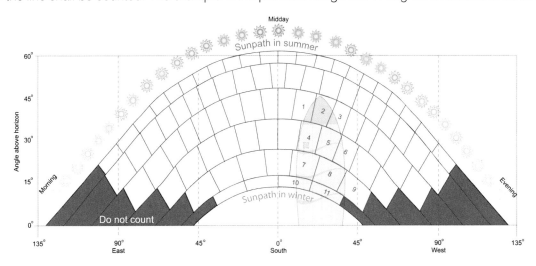

by or are under the horizon line as detailed in the next diagram.

From the MCS guide to installation of PV systems

The total number of segments are then multiplied by a value of 0.01 and the total value is then subtracted from 1. In the previous example this would be:

$$1 - (0.01 \times 11) = 1 - 0.11 = \mathbf{0.89}$$

For systems that have multiple inverters or inverters with a capability to track more than one MPP, it is acceptable to carry out a separate shade factor calculation for each sub array.

Where any shade factor exists (i.e. the shade factor is not 1), the following disclaimer should be attached to the quote:

"This shade assessment has been undertaken using the standard MCS procedure – it is estimated that this method will yield results within 10% of the actual energy generated for most systems."

Objects at or less than 10m away from the centre midpoint of the array

Objects which fall into this category (for example: vent pipes, chimney stacks, satellite dishes etc) can have a very significant impact on the system performance through shading which is produced. It should always be the first consideration of the installer to site the array elsewhere out of the shading zone or removing the objects, which are causing the shade effect.

The following procedure should be applied if there are any objects, which remain:

● A horizon line should be drawn as described in the previous example.

● In addition to this, any objects that are on the horizon line and closer than 10m to any part of the array, shall add a shade circle to the diagram. A circle should be drawn for each object that meets this criterion.

● The circle shall have a radius equal to the height of the object and the apex of the circle shall sit on the highest

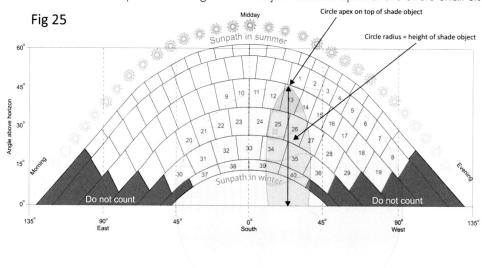

Fig 25

point of the object.

As with the previous example, any segments, which are touched or fall under the circle should be counted as part of the shade analysis.

As with the previous example, the number of segments are counted and multiplied by 0.01. The diagram indicates 40 segments touched by the shade circle. This would equate to:

$$1 - (0.01 \times 40) = 1 - 0.4 = \mathbf{0.6}$$

For an object, which has the same apex height but is at or less than 10m away from the array, the effect shade has on the system performance has caused a decrease of almost 30%. Ideally, there should be no shading at or less than 10m from the array to avoid this.

System performance calculation example

A system has been designed with a 3.5kWp output. The system is to be installed in Bristol with the array having a southern orientation and an inclination of 35°. There are 12 segments touched by the shade factor assessment carried out at the proposed site. Calculate the annual energy generated by the system.

The first step is to identify which table is to be used to give the Kk value for the equation. Bristol has been identified as the location for the system. Using the geographical map of the UK with the table numbers attached, table 5E should be utilised.

Having identified that 5E is the appropriate table, the next step is to identify the value of Kk by using the orientation and the angle of inclination. Having a southern orientation and an inclination angle of 35°, the value of Kk is 971.

Once this value has been identified, the shade factor must be calculated. The example has given the number of segments shaded as 12. The calculation would be:

$$1 - (0.01 \times 12) = 1 - 0.12 = \mathbf{0.88}$$

Now that all of the values have been calculated, these should be entered into the formula:

$$kWh/Year = kWp \times Kk \times SF = 3.5 \times 971 \times 0.88 = \mathbf{2990.7\ kWh/Year}$$

This value can be used to establish how much money can be earned through the feed-in tariff. Additional benefit would also include the offsetting of energy required from the grid as well as money generated through export of electricity to the grid.

As well as the requirement for estimation of system performance, there is also a requirement to calculate the wind and snow loading capabilities of the array and building structure calculations.

Wind and snow loading calculations

All information on wind and snow loading has been taken from the IET Code of Practice for Grid Connected Solar Photovoltaic Systems.

Wind Loading

A PV array and it's mounting structure and fixings require to be able to withstand additional forces exerted on them over the lifetime of the system. This would also apply to any structure that the array is affixed to. It is therefore necessary to consider the wind and snow loading for the particular site and system being designed.

Determining the wind loading on a system is performed to ensure that the mounting structure and fixings are sufficient to withstand any uplift, sliding and overturning that the wind loading will impose. Wind uplift calculations are required for specifying fixings for systems attached to buildings whereas sliding and overturning calculations would be required for ballasted systems.

The procedure for this involves two stages. The first is to determine the peak velocity pressure that the wind will impose at the site. The second involves converting this peak velocity pressure into a force by multiplying it by the area and the appropriate pressure coefficient:

1 - Wind force

$$\text{Wind force} = \textbf{QP x A x CP x SF}$$

Where:

QP = Peak Velocity Pressure

A = Area

CP = Pressure Coefficient

SF = Safety Factor

2 - Peak Velocity Pressure

Peak velocity pressure is the maximum wind pressure that is expected to be at a particular site over a 50-year-period. The procedure for calculating this is contained within BS EN 1991 Eurocode 1: Actions on structures and the UK National Annex: NA to BS EN 1991-1-4 – Eurocode 1: Actions on structures. General actions. Wind actions.

In order to calculate the peak velocity pressure, the following site factors need to be taken into account:

a) Basic mean wind velocity (which varies according to location – taken from a map of the UK);

b) Altitude correction factor (accounts for the height above sea level);

c) Reference height (height of the structure above ground level);

d) Terrain-roughness (terrain type: sea, town or country);

e) Topography – adds a correction factor where the site is on a hill or escarpment;

f) Distance from the sea.

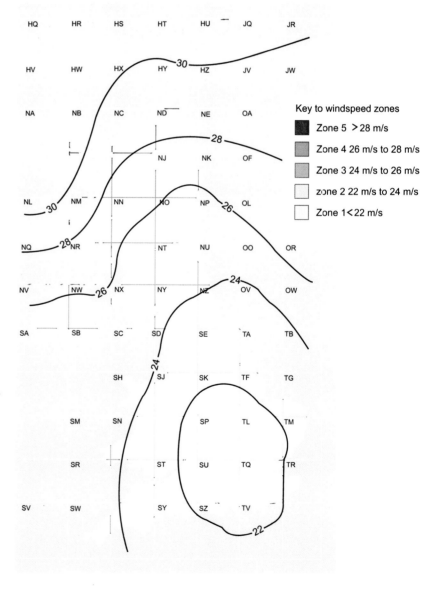

Key to windspeed zones

- ■ Zone 5 > 28 m/s
- Zone 4 26 m/s to 28 m/s
- Zone 3 24 m/s to 26 m/s
- Zone 2 22 m/s to 24 m/s
- □ Zone 1 < 22 m/s

A simplified method for calculating peak velocity pressure can be found in BRE DG 489 – Wind loads on roof mounted solar systems.

3 - Pressure coefficient

The pressure coefficient used in wind load calculations need to be selected according to the nature of the array mounting system.

BRE DG 489 provides information on the selection and use of pressure coefficients for PV arrays mounted on roofs. The document also provides guidance on the application of BS EN 1991 Eurocode 1 to PV systems.

It should be noted that pressure coefficients for arrays mounted on pitched or flat roofs shall be selected according to the requirements of BRE DG 489 and all other systems shall be taken from BS EN 1991 Eurocode 1. Forces on ground mounted systems may also be calculated using the flat roof procedure within BRE DG 489 and setting the building height to zero.

The selection of the appropriate pressure coefficient for a PV system mounted on a building also needs to take into consideration the relative location of the array on the building. Pressure coefficients within central zones will be lower than those at the building edges.

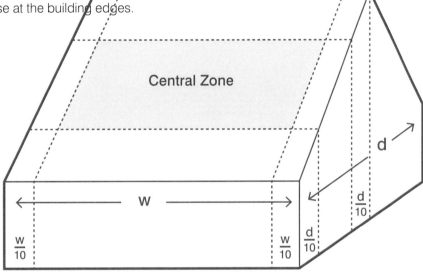

Example of central and edge zones (pitched roof) –
Courtesy of IET Code of Practice for Grid-Connected Solar Photovoltaic Systems

4 - Safety Factor

A safety factor needs to be applied in all wind load calculations in accordance with the requirements of BS EN 1991 Eurocode 1.

For PV systems mounted on roofs, a safety factor of 1.35 can typically be used, in accordance with the requirements of BRE DG 489.

It should be noted that the 1.35 factor is derived from a partial load factor of 1.5 (from BS EN 1991 Eurocode

1) multiplied by a consequence class factor (CC1) of 0.9 taken from BS EN 1990, Eurocode: Basis of structural design.

Wind load calculation example

System data:

a) Pitched roof – duopitch, 30°

b) Modules mounted above and parallel to roof

c) Array wholly in central area of roof

d) 16 panel system, each panel 1.6m²

e) Peak velocity pressure (Qp) = 763 Pa (calculated using BS EN 1991 Eurocode 1).

Area of the array: **A = 25.6m2 (16 x 1.6m2)**

Pressure Coefficients: **CP = -0.5 (From BRE DG 489 – Uplift)**

                                Cp = +0.26 (From BRE DG 489 – Down)

Safety Factor   **SF = 1.35 (From BRE DG 489)**

Total wind (uplift) force acting on the array $= Q_p \times A \times C_p \times SF$

$= 763 \times 25.6 \times 0.5 \times 1.35 = 13.18kN$

Total wind (uplift) force per module $= Q_p \times A \times C_p \times SF$

$= 763 \times 1.6 \times 0.5 \times 1.35 = 824N$

Total wind (down) force acting on the array $= Q_p \times A \times C_p \times SF$

$= 763 \times 25.6 \times 0.26 \times 1.35 = 6.86kN$

Total wind (down) force per module $= Q_p \times A \times C_p \times SF$

$= 763 \times 1.6 \times 0.26 \times 1.35 = 429N$

Snow Loading

Determining snow loads is performed primarily when looking at the suitability of a building structure to accept a PV array, for example, when considering the ability of roof trusses to accept the additional load of a PV array. Knowledge of snow loads may also be required when designing array frames or where the nature of the array design may trap and accumulate snow.

The procedure for determining snow loads within the UK is contained within BS EN 1991 Eurocode 1 and the UK National Annex: NA to BS EN 1991-1-3: Actions on structures. General actions. Snow loads.

Load calculations

1 – PV Module

The PV module shall be checked to ensure it can withstand the wind and snow loads calculated for the site.

Mechanical design is often only concerned with the array frame and fixings and the checking of the module rating is overlooked. In some high-wind-load applications, such as facades, the module may not be suitable for the loads which will be imposed.

2 – Array mounting frame

The PV array mounting frame shall be rated for the wind and snow loads calculated for the site.

The detailed mechanical design is not included on this course. While off-the-shelf mounting systems should have maximum loading specified by the manufacturer, this will not be the case for bespoke framing systems. In such cases, a suitably competent person will need to ensure that the bespoke mounting system is fit for purpose.

3 – Fixings

The fixings used to secure a PV system shall be rated for the wind and snow loads calculated for the site.

The fixings selected for a PV array need to be of a type and quantity able to withstand the loads imposed. In most cases, the key factor will be the wind uplift force. Fixings manufacturers will commonly supply a rated withstand value for each type of fixing (provided the installation instructions are followed). It is then a matter of ensuring that sufficient fixings are specified to withstand the calculated wind uplift.

Fixing calculation example

System data:

a) Total wind (uplift) force acting on the array = 13.18kN

b) Fixing bracket rated capacity = 500N (includes safety factor)

$$\text{Wind uplift/bracket capacity} = 13.18 \div 0.5 = \mathbf{26.36}$$

$$\text{Minimum number of fixings required} = \mathbf{27}$$

It's important to determine whether the fixing capacity provided by the manufacturer includes a safety factor (as this can vary between manufacturers). If no safety factor has been applied, an appropriate factor will need to be included as part of the fixing calculations.

Not only should the correct number of fixings be installed, but their layout and deployment must be suitable for the array frame and the structure it is connected to. For example, on a roof mounted system, the fixings will need to be spread appropriately across all the roof rafters beneath the array. Fixings also need to be suitable for the structure and material they are attached to.

4 – Building structure

The building structure shall be checked to ensure that it is able to withstand the imposed loads resulting from the installation of the PV system. Calculations shall be undertaken by a suitably competent person.

In general, the installation of a typical 'on-roof' PV system on a building will not increase the wind uplift forces on the building structure. However, the increased weight of the PV array system reduces the capacity of the structure to withstand the downwards-imposed wind and snow loads.

Before installing a PV system, it is necessary to ensure that there is sufficient residual capacity in the building structure to accept both the existing loads and the added weight of the PV system.

Detailed structural calculations are not included on this course.

Before fitting a PV system to an existing building, the building should be inspected by a suitably competent person to ensure that the existing structure is free from decay or any other factors that could jeopardise the suitability of the structure to accept the addition of a PV array.

The method of fixing shall also be reviewed to ensure that the fixings do not compromise the integrity of the timber or other structure to which they are attached.

Metering

Inverter output meter: As a minimum, metering at the inverter output should be installed to display/record energy delivered by the PV system (kWh). In addition it is highly recommended for instantaneous power output (kW) to be displayed. This is normally a display function of the inverter.

The meter should be located where the consumer can readily observe it. As detailed in the MCS Metering Guidance document, this would ideally be adjacent to the consumer unit of the property.

Building Export meter: Although not directly part of the PV system, where required in order to enable payment on exported electricity, an approved kWh export meter with appropriate reading capabilities may be required.

The appropriate Energy Supplier should be contacted to find out any particular requirements and to arrange for its fitting.

The UK government may introduce the Smart Export Guarantee for electrical energy which is exported to the grid. This would involve the installation of a smart meter to accurately measure the value of energy exported and could replace any building export meter which would not include the adequate features required for the incentive.

100A Electronic Single Phase Import/Export Meter
(Image courtesy of www.thepowerstore.co.uk)

Module 5

Commissioning and client hand-over

Module 5 – Commissioning and client hand-over

The commissioning of a PV system is required to ensure that the system is working and that it complies with the current regulations governing the equipment. There are several inspections and tests that are required to be carried out and documentation must be completed for the records of both the installer and the customer.

The following sequence should be observed:

1. Inspection

2. PV Testing

3. Current edition of ER G98 Verification

Inspection

As part of the inspection process to comply with the current edition of BS 7671 Part 6, a solar PV inspection checklist must be completed. Table 5.1 highlights the parts to be visually inspected to ensure that the installation has been installed correctly before any testing can be carried out:

Table 5.1 – Summary of inspection requirements

Item	Requirement	
DC system - general	a)	General check to confirm system complies with relevant standards.
	b)	PV voltage suitable for location.
	c)	Components selected and erected to suit location and external influences.
	d)	Roof and building penetrations weatherproof.
DC system – protection against shock	a)	Protective measures provided by extra low voltage (SELV/PELV).
	b)	Protection by use of class II or equivalent insulation.
	c)	Parts selected and erected so as to minimise the risk of earth faults and short-circuits.
DC system – protection against insulation faults	a)	Identification if the inverter has at least galvanic/simple separation.
	b)	Identification of functional earthing.
	c)	Presence of earth insulation resistance detection and alarm system.
	d)	Presence of earth residual current monitoring detection and alarm system.
DC system – protection against overcurrent	a)	$I_{MOD\_MAX\_OCPR}$ > possible reverse current.
	b)	Sting cables sized appropriately for prospective fault currents.
	c)	String/array overcurrent protective devices correctly specified and installed.
DC system – earthing and bonding arrangements	a)	Check of any functional earth connections.
	b)	Check functional earth fault interrupters are fitted (if required).
	c)	Check of the earthing and/or equipotential bonding of array frame.
	d)	Where protective earthing and/or bonding conductors are installed, they are parallel to, and bunched with, the DC cables.

DC system – protection against the effects of lightning and overvoltage	a)	Area of wiring loops is minimised.
	b)	Measures in place to protect long cables (screening or use of SPD's).
	c)	Surge Protection Devices (SPD's), where fitted, are suitably selected and erected.
DC system – selection and erection of electrical equipment	a)	All PV modules are rated for the maximum possible DC system voltage.
	b)	All DC components are rated for continuous DC operation, voltage and current maxima.
	c)	Wiring selected and erected to suit external influences (wind, UV, temperature etc).
	d)	String/array isolation and disconnection devices correctly specified and located.
	e)	DC switch disconnector is fitted to the DC side of the inverter.
	f)	Plug and socket connectors are of the same type, correctly mated and from the same manufacturer.
AC system	a)	A means of isolating the inverter has been provided on the AC side.
	b)	Isolators correctly connected.
	c)	Inverter parameters correctly specified.
	d)	RCD's correctly selected and installed (where fitted).
Labelling	a)	All parts correctly labelled and suitably durable:
	b)	Schematics and other signs suitable displayed.

PV inspection requirements table – Courtesy of IET Code of Practice for Grid-Connected Solar Photovoltaic Systems

As good practice, the installer should record module and inverter serial numbers not only for warranty purposes but the inverter serial number is required to be recorded on the documentation to be submitted to the Distribution Network Operator (DNO).

In order to progress to the commissioning stage of the installation, the inspection stage must be verified as being satisfactory; any areas where the pre-commissioning checklist is not ticked as satisfactory or N/A must be rectified before commissioning.

The labelling and identification are very important and all labels should be in the correct location, clear and easily readable. The labels must be suitably affixed and durable. Labelling should be provided at the servicing position, meter position and all points of isolation to indicate the presence of on-site generation and indicating the position of the main AC switch disconnector. On the next page is an example of an appropriate warning label to indicate the presence of two electricity supplies. Additional information on the labelling of PV systems is provided within the IET Code of Practice for Grid Connected Solar Photovoltaic Systems.

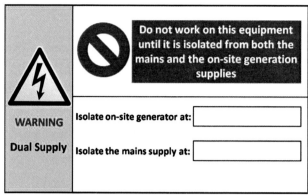

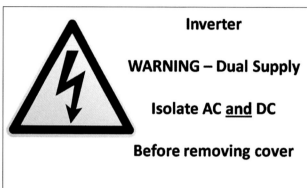

 Do not disconnect d.c. plugs and sockets under load- Turn off a.c.supply first.

 PV Array d.c. junction box. Danger contains live parts during daylight.

 PV Array d.c. isolator. Danger contains live parts during daylight.

 Inverter - Isolate a.c. and d.c. before carrying out work.

 PV system - Main a.c. isolator.

Dual supply label

Dual supply labelling should be provided at the service termination, meter position and all points of isolation between the PV system and supplier terminals to indicate the presence of on-site generation and indicating the position of the main a.c. switch disconnector.	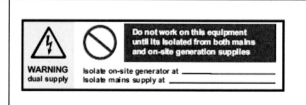

At any point of grid interconnection (distribution board or consumer unit), the following information should be displayed:

Circuit diagram & system information

At the point of interconnection, the following information is to be displayed (typically all displayed on the circuit diagram):

- Circuit diagram showing the relationship between the inverter equipment and supply.
- A summary of the protection settings incorporated within the equipment.
- A contact telephone number for the supplier/installer/maintainer of the equipment.
- It is also good practice for shutdown and start-up procedures to be detailed on this diagram.

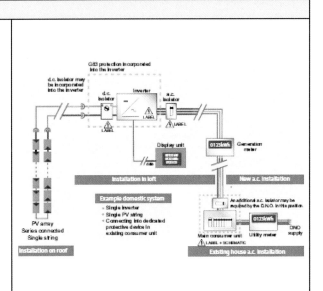

Fire and Rescue Notification

To ensure the Fire and Rescue Service are aware that a PV system is installed on the roof, the following sign shall also be fitted

- Location: next to the suppliers' cut-out in the building
- Size: This label shall measure at least 100mm x 100mm
- Only required for PV systems fitted on roofs

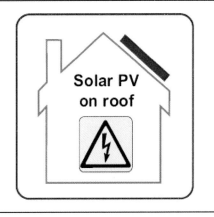

- Circuit diagram showing the relationship between the inverter equipment and the supply.

- A summary of the protection settings incorporated within the equipment.

- A contact telephone number for the supplier/installer/service operator of the equipment.

The above labelling and information were required to meet ER G83. However, EREC G98 has now replaced G83 and has listed the following labelling requirements:

- Labelling shall be placed in accordance with EN50438 (Dual supply labelling). This warning label does not imply a right on the customer, installer or maintainer to operate (remove/replace) the DNO's cut out fuse. A note to this effect should be included on the warning label.

- In addition to the warning label, EREC G98 requires the following, up to date, information to be displayed at the Connection Point with the DNO's Distribution Network.

  a) A circuit diagram relevant to the installation showing the circuit wiring, including all protective devices, between the Micro-generator and the DNO's fused cut-out. This diagram should also show by whom all apparatus is owned and maintained; and

  b) A summary of the Interface Protection settings incorporated within the Micro-generator.

- The Installer shall advise the Customer that it is the Customer's responsibility to ensure that this safety information is kept up to date. The installation operating instructions shall contain the Manufacturer's contact details e.g. name, telephone number and web address.

Testing

The testing of the PV system should be carried out prior to grid connection. The testing of the AC side of the PV system should be carried out to meet the requirements of the current edition of BS7671, Part 6 – Inspection and Testing. The testing of the DC side of the PV system should be carried out to meet the requirements of BS EN 62446. PV systems constructed of AC modules, power optimisers or with any other form of module level electronics should consult table 5.2 for modifications to required testing regimes.

Table 5.2 – Modifications to the testing regime for systems with module level electronics

System	Modifications to standard test regime
AC Module	- No DC test or inspection of works required.
Micro inverter No site construction wiring is used (all connections using module and inverter leads)	- Testing of DC circuits is not required. - Inspection of DC works is required.
Micro inverter Site constructed wiring is used	- Testing of DC circuits is required. - Inspection of DC works is required.
Module integrated electronics	- Where possible, a standard test regime to be followed. - Manufacturer to be consulted to determine any restrictions to tests. (e.g. insulation resistance test). - Manufacturer to be consulted on pass/fail criteria for tests (e.g. expected VOC).

Modification of testing regime table – Courtesy of BS EN 62446

A summary of the DC tests required as a minimum is listed on table 5.3.

Table 5.3 – Summary of minimum test requirements

Item	Requirement
Continuity of earthing and/or equipotential bonding conductors	a) Test to ensure the continuity of earthing and/or equipotential bonding conductors (if fitted). b) Connection to the main earthing terminal verified.
Polarity test	Test to ensure that all strings and arrays are correctly marked and connected.
Combiner (Junction) box test	Test to ensure that all strings are correctly connected within a combiner (junction) box (if fitted).
String open circuit voltage test	a) Test to ensure that there are no major faults within a string, b) Short-circuit and operational test options presented.

String circuit current test	a) Test to ensure that there are no major faults within a string,
	b) Short-circuit and operational test options presented.
Function tests	a) Tests to ensure switchgear operates correctly.
	b) Tests to ensure inverter/s operating correctly.
Insulation resistance of the DC circuits	Test of the insulation resistance of PV string and array circuits.

DC minimum testing requirement table – Courtesy of IET Code of Practice for Grid-Connected Solar Photovoltaic Systems.

In addition to the minimum sequence of tests outlined in the table above, an expanded sequence of tests may be required in certain circumstances, as detailed in BS EN 62446. As these tests are more suited to larger systems, a summary is given on table 5.4, but details of the tests will not be given on this course.

Table 5.4– Summary of additional tests

Item	Requirement
IV curve test	a) Will provide all key string parameters (V_{OC}, I_{SC}, V_{MPP}, I_{MPP}, P_{MAX}).
	b) Can help identify module/array defects or shading issues.
Infrared Inspection	a)1 Performed to detect abnormal module temperature variations and help identify problems such as bypass diode failures, hot spots, etc.
	b) Can also be performed on junction boxes and switchgear.
Voltage to ground	A test to evaluate functionally grounded systems using a high impedance connection.
Blocking diode test	Test to verify blocking diodes (if fitted).
Wet insulation resistance test	A variation on the standard insulation resistance test – typically only used during fault-finding exercises.
Shade evaluation	Recording shade conditions at date of installation.
	(It should be noted that MCS installations require a shade evaluation of the PV system. The details of this procedure are covered in the previous module and are better detailed than the procedure outlined in BS EN 62446.)

DC additional test table – Courtesy of IET Code of Practice for Grid-Connected Solar Photovoltaic Systems.

Guidance on how to carry out the tests listed in table 5.3 are given in the following sections. This information has been taken from BS EN 62446.

- **Continuity of protective earthing and equipotential bonding conductors**

  - Where protective earthing and/or equipotential bonding conductors are fitted on the DC side, such as bonding of the array frame, an electrical continuity test shall be made on all such conductors. The connection to the main earthing terminal should also be verified.

- **Polarity test**

  - The polarity of all DC cables shall be verified using suitable test apparatus. Once polarity is confirmed, cables shall be checked to ensure they are correctly identified and correctly connected into system devices such as switching devices or inverters.

  NOTE: For reasons of safety and for the prevention of damage to connected equipment, it is extremely important to perform the polarity check before other test and before switches are closed or string overcurrent protective devices are installed. If a check is made on a previously connected system and reverse polarity of one string is found, it is then important to check modules and bypass diodes for any damage caused by this error.

- **PV string combiner (junction) box test**

  A single string connected in reverse polarity within a PV string combiner (junction) box can sometimes be easy to miss. The purpose of the combiner (junction) box test is to ensure all strings interconnected at the combiner (junction) box are connected correctly.

  Polarity of PV strings may be tested by a digital multi-meter between positive and negative, or between one of the poles and ground, and checked that all the measured values are consistently positive and negative.

  When checking a large number of circuits, the appearance of the "-" symbol can be relatively easy to overlook. The alternative method detailed below may also be used, and should only be used where the meter being used for the tests has a range of at least twice V_{oc}.

  - **Test procedure**

  The test procedure is as follows and shall be performed before any string fuses/connectors are inserted for the first time:

  - Select a voltmeter with a voltage range at least twice the maximum system voltage.

  - Insert all negative fuses/connectors so strings share a common negative bus.

  - Do not insert any positive fuses/connectors.

  - Measure the open circuit voltage of the first string, positive to negative, and ensure it is an expected value.

  - Leave one lead on the positive pole of the first string tested and put the other lead on the positive pole of the next string. Because the two strings share a common negative reference, the voltage measured should be near-zero, with an acceptable tolerance range of ± 15V.

  - Continue measurements on subsequent strings, using the first positive circuit as the meter common connection.

  - A reverse polarity condition will be very evident if it exists – the measured voltage will be twice the system voltage.

- **PV string – Open circuit voltage measurement**

  The open circuit voltage of each PV string should be measured using suitable measuring apparatus. This should be done before closing any switches or installing string overcurrent protective devices (where fitted). Ideally, this would be carried out at a DC switch disconnector or combiner (junction) box.

  The resulting string open circuit voltage reading shall then be assessed to ensure it matches the expected value (typically within 5%) in one of the following ways:

- Compare with the expected value derived from the module datasheet or from a detailed PV model that considers the type and number of modules and the module cell temperature (M x V_{OC} for a single module).

- Measure VOC on a single module, then use this value to calculate the expected value for the string (most suitable where there is stable irradiance conditions).

- For systems with multiple identical strings and where there are stable irradiance conditions, voltages between strings can be compared.

- For systems with multiple identical strings and where there is non-stable irradiance conditions, voltages between strings can be compared using multiple meters with one meter on a reference string.

PV string – Current measurement

Two test methods are possible (short circuit test or operational test) and both will provide information on the correct functioning of the PV string. Where possible, the short circuit test is preferred as it will exclude any influence from the inverter/s. For the purposes of this course, we will only cover the short circuit current test.

The short circuit current of each PV string should be measured using suitable test apparatus. The making/ interruption of string short circuit currents is potentially hazardous, and a suitable test procedure should be followed.

The measured values should be compared with either the value from an adjacent identical string or from a calculated expected value. A calculated value can be obtained for the module manufacturer's IV curves (selecting the appropriate curve for the irradiation conditions at the time of the test) or calculated from the manufacturer's data (normalizing the current at 1000W/m2 to the measured irradiance).

In general, the measured value should be within ± 10% of the expected value. Where the difference is > 10%, a visual appraisal of the sunlight conditions may be used to consider the validity of the current readings; the string should also be investigated for any obvious issues such as shading, damage or installation defects.

Test Procedure

The procedure for carrying out the short circuit current test is as follows:

Ensure that all switching devices and disconnecting means are open and that all PV strings are isolated from each other.

A temporary short circuit shall be introduced into the string under test. This can be achieved by one of the following techniques:

a) Use of a test instrument with a short circuit current measurement function (e.g. a specialized PV tester);

b) A short circuit cable temporarily connected into a load break switching device (for example, a load break DC switch disconnector) already present in the string circuit;

c) Use of a "short circuit switch test box" – a load break rated device that can be temporarily introduced into the circuit to create a switched short circuit.

It should be noted that if option b) is selected, the short circuit cable should be connected to the load side of the load break switching device, i.e NOT the PV array connected side.

Once a suitable choice of short circuit connection has been chosen from the previous list, the following procedure is used to obtain a measured value of short circuit current:

- The test instrument shall have a rating greater than the potential short circuit current and open circuit voltage. Where a switching device and/or short circuit conductor is used to form the short circuit, these shall be rated greater than the potential short circuit current and open circuit voltage.

- The short circuit current can then be measured using a suitable rated clip-on ammeter, in-line ammeter or test instrument with a short circuit current measurement function. A simultaneous reading of the in-plane irradiance (W/m²) should be taken.

- The short circuit current shall then be interrupted using the load break switching device and the current checked to have gone to zero before any other connections are changed.

- The measure value of short circuit current should be compared to the calculated value. This can be done by dividing the measured value of short circuit current by the measure value of in-plane irradiance (W/m²) and then multiplied by 1000. This will normalise the measured value of short circuit current to STC irradiance conditions – 1000W/m².

$$\text{Normalised Isc} = \frac{\text{Measured Isc}}{\text{Measured in - plane irradiance}} \times 1000$$

- **Function Tests**

  The following function tests shall be performed:

  - Switchgear and other control apparatus shall be tested to ensure correct operation and that they are properly mounted and connected.

  - All inverters forming part of the PV system shall be tested to ensure correct operation. The test procedure should be defined by the inverter manufacturer.

  Functional tests that require AC supply to be present (e.g. inverter tests) shall only be performed once the AC side of the system has been tested.

- **PV array insulation resistance test**

  PV array DC circuits are live during daylight and, unlike a conventional AC circuit, cannot be isolated before performing this test.

  Performing this test presents a potential electric shock hazard; therefore, it is important to fully understand the procedure before starting any work. The following basic safety measures should be followed:

  - Limit the access to the working area.

  - Do not touch and take measures to prevent any other persons from touching any metallic surface when performing the insulation test

  - Do not touch and take measures to prevent any other persons from touching the back of the module/laminate or the module/laminate terminals when performing the insulation test.

  - Whenever the insulation test device is energised, there is voltage on the testing area. The equipment shall have automatic auto-discharge capability.

  - Appropriate personal protective clothing/equipment should be worn for the duration of the test.

  Where SPD's or other equipment are likely to influence the verification test, or be damaged, such equipment shall be temporarily disconnected before carrying out the insulation resistance test.

  The test should be repeated, as a minimum, for each of the PV array or sub-array (as applicable). It is also possible to test individual strings if required. There are two methods available to test the insulation resistance of the system:

- Test method 1 – Test between array negative and earth followed by a test between array positive and earth.

- Test method 2 – Test between earth and short-circuited array positive and negative.

Where the structure/frame is bonded to earth, the earth connection may be to any suitable earth connection or to the array frame (where the array frame is used, ensure good contact and that there is continuity over the whole metallic frame).

For systems where the array frame is not bonded to earth (e.g. where there is class II installation) a commissioning engineer may choose to do two tests: i) between array cables and earth and an additional test ii) between array cables and frame.

Where test method 2 is adopted, to minimise the risk from electrical arcs, the array positive and negative cables should be short-circuited in a safe manner. Typically, this would be achieved by an appropriate short-circuit switch box. Such a device incorporates a load break rated DC switch that can safely make and break the short circuit connection – after array cables have been safely connected into the device.

- **Test Procedure**

The test procedure should be designed to ensure peak voltage does not exceed module, switch, surge arrestor or other system component ratings.

Before commencing the test:

- Limit access by non-authorised personnel;

- Isolate the PV array from the inverter (typically at the array switch disconnector); and

- Disconnect any piece of equipment that could have impact on the insulation measurement (i.e. overvoltage protection) in the junction or combiner boxes.

The insulation resistance test device shall be connected between earth and the array cable(s) or combiner (junction) bus bar – as appropriate to the test method adopted. Test leads should be made secure before carrying out the test.

Follow the insulation resistance test device instructions to ensure the test voltage is in accordance with table 5.5 and readings in megaohms.

Ensure the system is de-energised before removing test cables or touching any conductive part.

Table 5.2 – Modifications to the testing regime for systems with module level electronics

System voltage (VOC (stc) x 1.25) V	Test Voltage V	Minimum insulation resistance MΩ
<120	250	0.5
120 to 500	500	1
>500 to 1000	1000	1
>1000	1500	1

Modification of testing regime table – Courtesy of BS EN 62446

The final stage of commissioning a PV system is that the inverter protection settings comply with the current edition of EREC G98. Although assurance is sought from the inverter manufacturer or supplier that the product is the current edition of EREC G98 compliant, this has still to be confirmed. This is usually carried out using a computer to interface with the inverter. Once the computer is connected, the installer can then set up a password and check the inverters protection settings. Start-up and shutdown times can be checked and 'anti-islanding' can be confirmed by setting the voltage to lower than grid value.

AC testing

The installation of the AC side of a PV system is no different to that of any electrical installation and therefore an electrical installation certificate shall be provided on completion in accordance with the current edition of BS 7671. The inspection and test schedules of the electrical installation certificate should be completed at the commissioning stage, although it is good practice to continually inspect and test installations throughout the duration of the installation.

The inspection schedule should be completed as per the current edition of BS 7671 and further reference to procedures can be found in IET Guidance Note 3. On completion of the inspection schedules the relevant tests should be carried out to verify that the installation complies with the current edition of BS 7671. The sequence of tests is as follows:

Dead tests

- Continuity of protective conductors

- Insulation resistance (apply caution to level of test voltage)

- Polarity

Live tests

- Earth fault loop impedance

- Prospective fault current

- RCD testing (if applicable)

- Functional testing

- Verification of voltage drop

As the installation will have equipment that may be damaged by test voltages during insulation resistance testing, the equipment should be disconnected from the test to avoid damage to the electrically sensitive equipment. The current edition of BS 7671, Reg. 643.3.2 states that if disconnection of the electrically sensitive equipment is not reasonably practicable then it is permissible to reduce the voltage from 500V DC to 250V DC.

If the inverter and all AC components are located close to the consumers unit or distribution board then it is likely that the voltage drop will be insignificant if the cables are correctly specified.

Documentation

There are a number of documents to be filled in when recording results for and certifying a PV system.

A comprehensive list of all documents required for PV systems can be found further on in this section.

Copies of the BS 7671 forms – Appendix 6 (Electrical Installation Certificate, Schedule of Inspections and Schedule of Test Results) must be completed for the installation.

An array-testing sheet should also be completed.

For individual small systems, the DNO must be notified within 28 days of the system connection. For a group of small systems, an 'Application for connection' form (an example of which is given in the current edition of EREC G98, appendix 3) must be used to formally apply to the DNO. The DNO may make some charge for investigating the likely impacts of the proposed systems on the electricity distribution network. If the application is approved by the DNO, they must be notified within 28 days of the system being commissioned.

For all systems, an 'Installation Document for connection under G98' (an example of which is given in the current edition of EREC G98, appendix 3) must be used to formally notify the DNO within 28 days of commissioning.

After the commissioning stage has been completed, a handover of the documentation should take place between the installer and the client. Before this takes place however, the installer should carry out pre-handover checks. These would include:

- All tools and access equipment has been removed.

- That all equipment opened or exposed during inspection and testing has been returned to an operational condition.

- Completion of PV checklist and Schedule of Inspections. Note: both of these documents should not have any crosses or limitations marked next to any item on the list as these documents are being used to complete an initial verification.

- Completion of PV array test results and a Schedule of Test results.

- Completion of Electrical Installation Certificate.

- Completion of pro-forma as required for either current edition of G83 or current edition of G59.

- All equipment and installer documentation is available to pass over to the client.

- Any deviations from original schematic diagram are noted and recorded.

The IET Code of Practice for Grid Connected Solar Photovoltaic Systems stipulates that the system user should be part of a handover process. This process should include:

a) Identifying parts of the installation and explaining their function;

b) Identifying health and safety considerations (in operation and maintenance stages);

c) Demonstrating 'normal' operation and explaining how to spot faults/poor performance;

d) Explaining any maintenance requirements and procedures;

e) Handing over the system manuals, drawings, test certificates and other associated paperwork; and

f) Answering client questions.

Handover procedures can vary significantly and need to tailored to the site in question. For some installations, certification scheme requirements may also apply.

The IET Code of Practice for Grid Connected Solar Photovoltaic Systems also stipulates that the system user should be provided with the information as described in BS EN 62446. The following tables (5.6-5.10) provide information on the documentation to be provided:

Table 5.6 – PV system documentation – Basic data

Item	Notes
System designer	Name, address and contact details.
System installer	Name, address and contact details.
Basic system infor-mation	a) Power rating of array and inverters. b) Make, model and quantity of key components (modules, inverters etc.). c) Installation and commissioning dates. d) Customer and site details.
Datasheets	Module and inverter datasheets

PV basic data table – Courtesy of IET Code of Practice for Grid-Connected Solar Photovoltaic Systems.

Table 5.7 – Test and commissioning data

Item	Notes
PV array	Array test results and certificates (BS EN 62446).
AC system	AC circuit test results and certificates (BS 7671).
G98/99 protection	a) Test results and certificates. b) Settings.
HV systems	Commissioning data, tests and results.

Test and commissioning data table – Courtesy of IET Code of Practice for Grid-Connected Solar Photovoltaic Systems.

Table 5.8 – PV array – Documentation scope

Item	Notes
Wiring diagrams	a) Wiring diagrams of all parts of the DC system. b) Identify which strings/array connects to which inverter(s).
PV string	a) Information on string configurations (module type and quantities). b) String cable details. c) Overcurrent protection details (including location and rating). NOTE: String information may be provided via the wiring diagram.
Array (and sub-arrays)	a) Information on array configuration (string type and quantities). b) Array cable details. c) Combiner (junction) box and isolator details (including location and rating). d) Overcurrent protection details (including location and rating). NOTE: Array information may be provided via the wiring diagram.

Earthing and over-voltage protection	a) Details of earth and bonding conductors.
	b) Details of any connections to an LPS.
	c) Details of any SPDs.
Physical layout	a) Physical layout of array and string connections.
	b) Plan of any buried or hidden PV array cables.
	NOTE: This is provided for subsequent fault finding and is particularly important on larger systems (particularly those mounted on buildings where access to the rear of modules is difficult).
Mechanical	Details of the PV mounting system.

PV array documents table – Courtesy of IET Code of Practice for Grid-Connected Solar Photovoltaic Systems

Table 5.9 – AC system – Documentation scope

Item	Notes
Wiring Diagrams	a) Wiring diagrams of all parts of the AC system.
	b) Identify which strings/array connects to which inverter.
AC system	a) AC isolators – including location and rating.
	b) Overcurrent protection – including location and rating.
	c) RCDs – including location and rating.
Earthing and over-voltage protection	a) Details of earthing and bonding systems and conductors.
	b) Details of any connection to an LPS.
	c) Details of an SPDs.
G99 Protection	a) Type and location.
	b) Settings.
HV systems	a) a) Specifications of transformers and switchgear.
	b) Cable details and locations.
	c) Earthing arrangements.

AC system document table – Courtesy of IET Code of Practice for Grid-Connected Solar Photovoltaic Systems

Table 5.10 – Operation and maintenance data

Item	Notes
Manuals	a) Inverter.
	b) PV modules.
	c) Data-loggers/displays.
Warranty	Warranty start date, duration and details.
Normal operation	a) How to verify 'normal' operation.
	b) Explanation of any alarm/error messaging systems.
Shutdown	Emergency isolation/shutdown procedures.

Fault-finding	a) Fault finding procedure.
	b) Service/emergency contact numbers.
Maintenance	a) Periodic maintenance/cleaning requirements.
	b) Service/inspection intervals.
	c) Information on any maintenance contracts.

Operation and maintenance table – Courtesy of IET Code of Practice for Grid-Connected Solar Photovoltaic Systems

Under the MCS scheme, a performance estimate, which gives a total annual AC energy output of a system. This shall be communicated to the client before the awarding of any contract. Sun path diagrams and any information used to calculate the performance estimate shall be given to the client as illustrated in the following table.

A. Installation data	
Installed capacity of PV system – kWp (stc)	kWp
Orientation of the PV system – degrees from South	°
Inclination of system – degrees from horizontal	°
Postcode region	
B. Calculations	
kWh/kWp (Kk) from table	kWh/kWp
Shade factor	
Estimated annual output (kWp x Kk x SF)	kWh

One or more of the following disclaimers shall accompany all quotes and/or estimates to customers.

For all quotations and/or estimates:

"The performance of solar PV systems is impossible to predict with certainty due to the variability in the amount of solar radiation (sunlight) from location to location and from year to year. This estimate is based upon the standard MCS procedure is given as guidance only. It should not be considered as a guarantee of performance."

Additionally where data has been estimated or taken remotely:

"This system performance calculation has been undertaken using estimated values for array orientation, inclination or shading. Actual performance may be significantly lower or higher if the characteristics of the installed system vary from the estimated values."

Additionally where the shade factor is less than 1:

"This shade assessment has been undertaken using the standard MCS procedure – it is estimated that this method will yield results within 10% of the actual energy generated for most systems."

Module 6

Maintenance and fault finding

Module 6 – Maintenance and fault finding

Maintenance and fault finding

As a general rule, PV arrays are normally fault free and very low maintenance. However, periodic maintenance checks should be carried out either by the system operator or the installer of the system to ensure that it continues to work efficiently and avoid potential faults. This is also a possible source of additional income for installers, who can offer maintenance contracts to the client. In the following module, the key points of a PV system will be looked at including checking and maintaining PV systems and possible remedy of any faults that may occur.

Maintaining a Solar Array
(Image courtesy of www.pasolar.ncat.org)

Maintenance

The following steps are only basic guidelines for common systems. Ensure that the manufacturer's instructions are read on the maintenance of their equipment. Before opening any equipment/apparatus, ensure safe isolation procedures are carried out (if applicable).

To ensure a high level of maintenance is achieved, the following information should be made available:

- All relevant certification (BS 7671) including:

  - Electrical Installation Certificate/Installation Condition Report.

  - Schedule of Inspections.

  - Schedule of Test Results.

  - A diagram of the installation and location of key equipment.

  - When the system was installed.

  - Any alterations made to the system after the initial installation.

  - When the system was last serviced/inspected.

Before carrying out any maintenance work, a Schedule of Inspections should be undertaken.

Monthly

Meter reading

A log of the meter readings should be taken and monitored. (This may not be applicable with systems for automatic recording and evaluating of operating data.)

The following checks should be carried out at the module/array:

- Remove all sources of shade on the array and rinse the array to remove the built up dust, dirt and other debris. This may require additional time to remove bird droppings or tree sap.

Annually

PV junction box

The junction box should be opened to inspect the connections. Also check for any insects or foreign bodies, signs of humidity and check fuses (if applicable). Use a voltmeter and DC ammeter to measure and record the array's operating voltage and current level on the output side of the junction box. Note the irradiance level at the time. Remove the fuses (if applicable) and record each string's Open-Circuit Voltage and current levels. Note any deviation between strings for future correction. You can also use these measurements to determine if the array's output is degrading over time.

PV array surface area

- Record the condition of the modules. Look for signs of degradation (this would include colour changes, fogged glazing, de-lamination, warping or water leaks etc), cracked glazing and the module frames being bent.

- All nuts and bolts for the array frame and modules should be checked and tightened as required.

- Loose cabling from the modules should be secured and checked for degradation or damage from wildlife or adverse weather. Check for any cuts, gashes or worn spots and replace as necessary. Check all the connections between the modules are tight and have no damage done to any shrouds or connectors. Replace as necessary.

- Check the frame earthing connections (if applicable).

- Check the building penetrations for adequate sealing and repair as required.

- Open the junction boxes and look for any dirty, loose or broken connections. Repair or replace as required. Check all connections inside the junction box and tighten as necessary.

Inverter

The following checks should be carried out at the inverter:

- A voltmeter and DC ammeter should be used to check and record the inverters operating DC input voltage and current level. The same should apply to the AC output.

- Check the functionality of the inverter; ensure that LED's are in working order, readouts are working and displaying appropriate information.

- Record the total kWh produced since first start up (if possible). Use the readout to compare the systems production between inspections.

- Isolate the inverter and check for loose, dirty or broken connections. Check the casing for cracks or damage. Switch the inverter on and ensure that the start up operation is normal and that it is producing AC Electricity.

Every three to four years

A repeat of the commissioning measurements

This must only be carried out by trained personnel.

Inverters in outdoor applications

Check the inverter for signs of humidity or water penetration regardless of suitability for outdoor conditions.
This must only be carried out by trained personnel.

The following checks should be employed if there is reason to suspect a fault.

If suspected

Modules, junction boxes and AC protective equipment

Peak output measurements should be taken. This must only be carried out by trained personnel. String fuses should be checked along with circuit breakers and RCD's.

Maintenance

Maintenance is a fundamental requirement of The Electricity At Work Regulations 1989. Although the regulations do not specifically state how this should be done for electrical installations, the current edition of BS 7671 provides further guidance on how to comply with this requirement. The requirement to maintain electrical systems involves keeping records of maintenance.

The recording and reporting of maintenance is an essential process of keeping accurate and up-to-date information on the PV system. The company/competent person carrying out the maintenance should have a method of recording any measurements or conditions that are taken or observed. The measurements and observations should be used to construct a condition report, giving all details of the maintenance procedure and any recommendations for repairing or replacing faulty or inadequate equipment. The customer should receive a copy of the report once it has been completed.

It is regarded as good practice to regularly check the inverter fault display on a daily basis, if possible. If the system has automatic fault and operating data monitoring, this can make the system operator's task much easier should a fault occur.

Additional information on the maintenance and operation of PV systems can be found in the IET Code of Practice for Grid Connected Solar Photovoltaic Systems.

Troubleshooting

A PV system is expected to operate between 25 and 30 years. Due to exposure to the weather, various faults can occur within this time. Depending on the fault, it is always advisable that a visual check be carried out first, particularly of the PV array. Mechanical damage and soiling should be looked for and all wiring connections should be checked.

The following information should be made available when diagnosing and rectifying any faults:

- All relevant certification (BS 7671) including:

  - Electrical Installation Certificate/Installation Condition Report.

  - Schedule of Inspections.

  - Schedule of Test Results.

- A diagram of the installation and location of key equipment.

- When the system was installed.

- Any alterations made to the system after the initial installation.

- When the system was last serviced/inspected.

- The nature of the fault/how often it occurs/what happens to the system.

When troubleshooting a grid-connected PV system, common diagnosis includes:

- The inverter does not operate properly or not at all; or

- The array has low or no voltage/current

Inverter problems

A lack of power output from the inverter could be caused by a blown string fuse, broken cable, an earth fault or any of the inverters internal disconnection tolerances (high and low voltage/current values).

With the inverter switched off (using the AC switch disconnector) check for and repair any earth faults before starting the inverter. Check for blown string fuses and replace as appropriate.

Fluctuations in the conditions affecting the array can alter the DC voltage/current values and if these are not within the inverters tolerances, this can cause the inverter to shut down.

Array problems

Before looking at the array itself, measure and record the inverters input voltage/current level from the array. If there is no DC voltage/current value at the inverter, check all DC components. Check for any loose/broken cabling in the inverter. Replace damaged cabling, clean and tighten all terminations.

The array should be visibly checked for obvious damage to the modules or cabling. Repair and replace all damaged cabling as required.

If the output voltage is low, this would indicate that some modules in a series string are defective or disconnected and may need replaced. Blocking diodes (if applicable) may also be defective and need replacing.

Low current output could be caused by the conditions of the weather (cloudy), defective blocking diodes, damaged module, parallel connections between strings may be broken, loose or dirty. Replace any faulty modules and defective diodes. Clean and tighten any loose connections. Any sources of shading should be removed from the area of the array. Heavy soiling must also be removed.

The measurements required to find faults in a grid-connected system are essentially the same as those required for the commissioning of the system. Therefore, the fault-finding process should be taken from the testing procedure in Module 5.

Fault finding

Some examples of common faults are listed below.

- Loss of full collection capacity

- Loss of output from inverter

- Loss of AC supply circuit to inverter

- No output from DC circuit

- Broken or damaged solar module

- Cable failure within DC circuit

- Dirty/partially covered/shaded modules

In order to diagnose these faults, a logical step-by-step process should be considered. There are some general guidelines which could apply to all of these faults which could be timesaving.

1. Ask the person responsible for the system what the fault is. This can also extend to aspects of the fault, such as, how often the fault occurs? Does the fault occur at certain times of day? Has the system been regularly maintained?

2. Carry out a visual inspection of all the equipment including the PV array. Some faults can occur due to perhaps a build up of dust or some shading of the array which would not require the need for access equipment to the roof and can be easily seen from ground level.

3. Carry out safety and functional testing of the system. If you know what it is supposed to do at various stages of operation it is reasonably easy to tell where and what is at fault.

These points should be the starting point of any fault diagnosis.

Specific diagnosis of the faults above would be as follows:

- **Loss of collection capacity** – Having taken steps 1 to 3 above, the next step would be to record the output readings of the array at the inverter. These should be checked against the expected values for both the voltage and current output of the array. Shading could have occurred or a string cable could be loose or disconnected. There is also the possibility (if the array has four or more strings) that a string fuse has blown. These would result in a loss of a string which would decrease the power output of the array.

- **Loss of output from the inverter** – Having taken steps 1 to 3 above, the next step would be to check the display of the inverter. This display should indicate whether there is an output coming from the array and if the inverter is receiving an AC signal. If either of these inputs are not apparent, see the other faults listed here for guidance on diagnosis. If both signals are present, this may indicate an internal failure of the inverter or that the input characteristics of the inverter (voltage/current) from the PV array are not being met.

- **Loss of AC Supply circuit to the inverter** – Having taken step 1 above, the fault should be easily identified. Check the display on the inverter, which should display a fault message indicating that there has been a loss of AC input. (This is part of the anti-islanding requirements specified as part of the current edition of G83). This could indicate loss of supply from the grid or could simply be that the MCB/RCD/AC switch-disconnector could have been switched off.

- **No output from DC circuit** – After carrying out step 1, the fault should be easily identifiable. Check the display on the inverter, which should indicate that there has been a loss of supply from the PV array. There are many reasons for this type of fault: Main DC cable loose or disconnected, complete shading of the entire array, string fuses have been blown or simply that the DC switch-disconnector has been switched off.

- **Broken or damaged solar module** – Carry out steps 1 to 3 above. There may need to be a comprehensive visual check done on the PV array which may require access equipment. The indication of this fault would be very similar to the first fault, where the damaged or broken module may result in a string not producing any power and loss of total collection capacity, indicated on the inverter display.

- **Cable failure within DC circuit** – Having carried out steps 1 to 3 above, the indication of this fault can either be reduced collection capacity or no output from the DC circuit which would be shown on the inverter display. There is also the chance that some panels may still continue to function and so the PV system should be turned off. Reduced collection would indicate that there would be either a loose connection or cable damage to a string cable whereas no output from the array would indicate the same fault but on a main DC cable.

- **Dirty/partially covered/shaded modules** – Having carried out steps 1 and 2 above, the indication of this fault can either be reduced collection capacity or no output from the DC circuit which would be shown on the inverter display. This type of fault is usually fairly simple to identify but shading is a little more difficult on cloudy or rainy days so you will have to imagine the passage of the sun. If the problem has occurred slowly it may be because no maintenance has been carried out or nearby trees have grown or new building has taken place. If it has occurred suddenly it may be fallen branches or wind blown materials that have landed on the modules.

Fault rectification

To rectify the faults given previously, we must diagnose the cause of the fault. Once this has been discovered, the following methods of rectifying these faults should be carried out:

- **Loss of collection capacity** – If shading has occurred, remove the object which is causing the shading effect (a well designed system should not have a permanent object which would cause regular shading effects on the PV array, such as a tree line or adjacent building). Check all connections and tighten or replace as appropriate. Replace any blown string fuses.

- **Loss of output from the inverter** – If internal failure of the inverter has occurred, the inverter must either be repaired (by a trained/competent person) or replaced. If the input characteristics are not within the inverter range, this maybe an indication of another fault present, such as broken or damaged module or DC cable failure, resulting in a reduced voltage/current output from the inverter. These will be rectified later in this list.

- **Loss of AC supply circuit to the inverter** – There are not many options open to rectifying this type of fault. Ensure that all points of switching and isolation are turned on. If this does not solve the problem, check the AC wiring from the consumer unit/distribution board to the inverter. The fault may have arisen from the loss of AC supply from the distributor, meaning that there is no rectification that can be carried out on the installed system.

- **No output from DC circuit** – Check that the DC switch-disconnector is in the ON position. Remove any objects causing the shading effect and tighten or replace any connections. Replace any blown string fuses.

- **Broken or damaged solar module** – There is no other way of rectifying this fault other than to replace the broken or damaged module. Please note that this string will be taken out of the array whilst the replacement is to be installed and simply connecting the two modules either side of the broken module should not be carried out. This would cause the string to be operating at a different voltage to any other strings on the array.

- **Cable failure within DC circuit** – Replacement of the cable that has failed is the only method of rectifying this fault.

- **Dirty/partially covered/shaded modules** – Depending on what has caused the problem this will be easy or could be difficult to resolve. If it is lack of maintenance i.e. build up of dirt or debris on the modules or fallen branches or plastic bags blown onto the array etc., simply cleaning them or removing the debris should solve the problem. Shading could be more difficult to cure as it may involve other people's property such as cutting branches of neighbour's trees and so on. If recent building is now causing shading it may be that the only solution is to relocate the array.

Module 7

PV Installation and Battery Storage Systems

Updated Material 2019

PV Installation and Battery Storage Systems

Introduction

Solar farm with battery storage - Courtesy of EnergyAustralia

In the past, battery storage systems were only installed in conjunction with PV systems for stand-alone applications which operated independently from the grid. However, with the withdrawal of the feed-in tariff and the increasing cost of buying electricity from the grid, battery storage systems are now being installed with new PV installations as well as being retro fitted to existing PV systems. It should be noted that the content within this section is not a design guide for battery storage but information on these systems and their relevance to PV systems.

There are three main reasons for considering the installation of a battery storage system with a grid-connected PV system:

a) To store electricity to be used/exported later in the day:

This is installed to allow the system operators to increase their self-consumption of generated electrical energy. Essentially, the system works by storing excess energy produced by the PV system during times where there is low electrical load requirement (normally during the day when people are at work/out and there a few electrical loads being used) and utilising the stored energy later that day when the energy being produced by the PV system has declined (when people come home from work and start using electrical equipment). This is also known as time-shifting. It can also facilitate the exporting of electrical energy to times when export tariffs are higher.

b) To limit the amount of electricity exported to the grid:

If a limit applies to the exporting of electrical energy from a specific PV system, battery storage could be installed at that site to allow a larger PV system to be installed. If the generated electrical energy from the PV system were to exceed the export limit imposed on the site, any additional energy could be diverted to the battery system and used on site.

c) To provide a back-up system for times of grid failure:

For the previous two reasons, the battery storage system would be relatively small and would only require to hold enough energy to run small electrical loads for a short period of time. However, the requirements of battery storage to replace an electrical supply in the event of grid failure are significantly different. They will normally be much larger in capacity due to longer storage periods, prolonged operation and will need to take into consideration the loads they are expected to supply.

The inverter-charger rating must also be considered. A system which is required to supply electrical energy in the event of grid failure may need a larger rating due to a potential in the increased loading it will have to run.

While providing additional functionality, the addition of battery storage to a grid-connected PV system needs careful consideration. A number of key factors to be considered are:

- Battery characteristics

- Capacity of the battery system (use and requirements)

- Configuration of the battery system (DC coupled or AC coupled)

- Battery system operation (time-shifting, backup, etc)

Battery characteristics

Any battery system will have a number of key characteristics that will impact on the operation, design and component selection.

Nominal capacity

This is, in effect, a value for the amount of electrical energy the battery can supply when fully charged, under a certain set of conditions.

The performance of a battery will be change depending on how it is charged and discharged, the environmental conditions it is installed in, the number of cycles (charging and discharging) the battery has been subjected to and the depth of discharge the manufacturer has designed the battery for. It is key to understand these conditions and how this relates to the nominal capacity value.

Battery capacity is normally given in Amp hours (Ah) at a particular discharge current, for example 200Ah at C100 rate (a rate of C100 equates to the current that will completely discharge the battery in 100 hours). The C-rate can have a significant effect on the battery capacity. When comparing the Ah rating of different batteries, check C-rate values to ensure an accurate comparison.

C-rate

As discussed, the is to enable a simple comparison between batteries. The discharge current from a battery is expressed in terms of a C-rate. This normalises the discharge current relative to the battery capacity.

- A rate of C1 equates to the current that will completely discharge the battery in one hour:

  - A battery rated at 500Ah at the rate of C1 means a discharge current of 500A for one hour (500 ÷ 1).

- A rate of C20 equates to the current that will completely discharge the battery in twenty hours:

  - A battery rated at 200Ah at the rate of C20 means a discharge current of 10A for 20 hours (200 ÷ 20).

Depth of discharge

Depth of discharge (DOD) gives information on how fully a battery has been discharged during a discharge profile and is given as a percentage of the battery capacity. A discharge of around 80% represents a deep cycle operation.

DOD can have a significant impact on the lifetime of a battery, especially for some technologies such as traditional lead-acid. The higher the DOD, the shorter the lifespan.

While lead-acid batteries are available for both shallow and deep cycles, lithium-ion batteries are generally all manufactured for deep cycle operation. Most lithium-ion batteries will be able to be discharged to 80% of nominal capacity without any significant effect on lifespan.

The number of life cycles varies depending on how deep the battery is discharged. Typically, the lower the DOD, the higher the number of battery cycles there are.

Effective capacity

It is common for a battery storage system to be programmed to limit the DOD and, therefore, limit the amount of capacity available for normal operation. The amount of capacity available for use by the system is normally termed 'effective capacity'. The effective capacity is less than the nominal capacity. This effectively means that, as a customer, you must "purchase" more battery kWh capacity than you will routinely use. For example:

- Nominal capacity: 500Ah

- System programmed DOD: 70% (0.7 as a factor)

$$\text{Nominal Capacity x DOD factor} = \text{Effective Capacity}$$
$$500 \times 0.7 = \mathbf{350Ah}$$

System efficiency (charge-discharge)

All batteries are subject to losses through the charging and discharging process. The efficiency of a battery can be expressed as the power out divided by the power in:

- Power in: 100kWh

- Power out: 80kWh

$$\text{Power out} \div \text{Power in} = \text{System Efficiency}$$
$$80 \div 100 = \mathbf{0.8\ (80\%)}$$

It should be noted however, that the efficiency of a battery storage system is not solely based on the efficiency of the battery but the complete battery storage system, taking into account the inverter charger also.

Conversion of Ah to kWh

Although battery capacity tends to be given in Amp hours (Ah), a number of manufacturers use Kilowatt hours (kWh) as a capacity value also.

To understand how each of these relate to one another, the following gives a method for conversion:

$$\text{Battery Voltage x Ah Rating} = \mathbf{Energy\ (kWh)}$$

For example:

- Amp hour rating: 500Ah

- Battery voltage: 12V

$$12 \times 500 = \textbf{6kWh (6000Wh)}$$

In certain circumstances, a battery with a lower Amp hour rating but a higher battery voltage may have a higher capacity, for example:

- Amp hour rating: 300Ah

- Battery voltage: 24V

$$24 \times 300 = \textbf{7.2kWh (7200Wh)}$$

Capacity of the battery system

The sizing of a battery storage system is important, primarily for two reasons:

1) Battery is too small: This would occur if the battery system cost is greater than the financial benefit from the stored power.

2) Battery is too large: This would occur if the battery system can't be fully charged with the exception of a few days per year.

In order to gauge the correct capacity of battery required for a system, a number of factors should be considered:

- PV and inverter sizing

- Load use

- Backup capacity

- Maximum charge/discharge rate

PV and inverter sizing

As battery size increases, the electrical energy produced by the PV system becomes insufficient to fully recharge the battery. The maximum daily output of electrical energy over the course of a year should be sought as a upper battery limit for capacity, where the system is to be used for self-consumption/time-shifting purposes.

Load use

The loads which the battery will be expected to supply will have a bearing on the system installed. Where a PV system is connected to an installation where loads are being used throughout the day, this will reduce the amount of generated electrical energy available to recharge the battery. This would have an impact on the capacity of battery required. If there were a small amount of loads used when the PV system is generating during the day, then the amount of generated electrical energy available to recharge the battery would increase. Once a battery has been fully charged, any further generated energy would either be used within the installation or would be exported to the grid.

Backup capacity

Where power is required during grid failure, a battery can either be partitioned so that some of its capacity is held in reserve or the total capacity is used for this purpose. This would depend on whether or not the battery is to be used purely as a backup source or as both a backup source and for time-shifting functionality also. If a battery is required to supply electrical energy to loads in the event of grid failure, a load evaluation would need to be performed. This evaluation would examine the power rating of the load/s to be supplied (in watts) and the duration the load requires the supply (in hours). A calculation would then be done to provide the energy required (in watthours). For example:

- Power rating for a light: 40w

- Duration required: 2 hours

Power Rating x Duration = Required Energy Storage

40 x 2 = **80Wh**

The example used however does not take into account any system losses (such as volt drop, heat loss etc). A multiplier should be used to take into account any expected losses. It would be the responsibility of the system designer to select an appropriate value for this but it is generally recommended that a figure of, at least, 1.1 (additional 10%) is used.

Power Rating x Duration x Multiplier = Required Energy Storage

40 x 2 x 1.1 = **88Wh**

Maximum charge-discharge rates

Charge and discharge rates are characteristics which would need to be considered when selecting a battery storage system. This relates directly to how much charge is acceptable for the battery to be subjected to whilst charging and how much charge the battery can export when loads demand.

The charging characteristic of the battery would be considered in conjunction with the PV inverter sizing and also the likelihood of loads being switched off during the PV system generating electrical energy, which would divert more energy from the PV system to the battery.

The discharge characteristic must consider which proportion of loads are to be supplied and could the battery meet these demands.

Where a battery system is used for self-consumption/time-shifting, it could be expected that, where a spike in energy is required (say for an electric shower), the battery's maximum discharge rate may not meet the required value but any shortfall could be imported from the grid. However, if the battery is required as a backup source in the event of grid failure, it may fail to meet these load demands. Consideration of which loads are required to be supplied in the event of grid failure and the maximum current required by these loads (taking into account surge currents) would be needed.

Configuration of the battery system

Grid-connected battery storage systems come in different forms depending on the manufacturer and their installation. Some systems will come as complete packages whilst others are designed and installed using a number of different components.

Regardless of this, it is important to understand the components which are involved in the system and how these are connected.

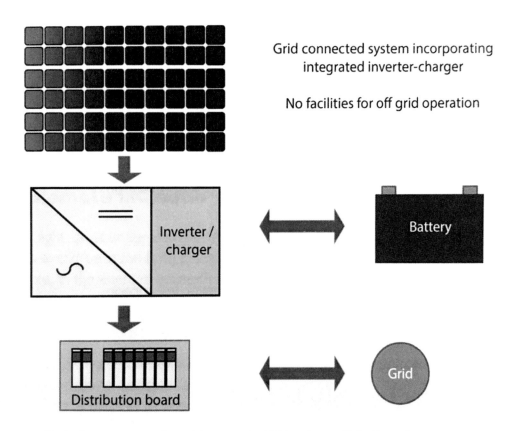

Grid connected system incorporating
integrated inverter-charger

No facilities for off grid operation

Typical arrangement for grid-connected PV system with battery storage -
Courtesy of IET Code of Practice for Grid-Connected Solar Photovoltaic Systems

The two main methods of connecting battery storage to a PV system is either by coupling this on the DC side or the AC side.

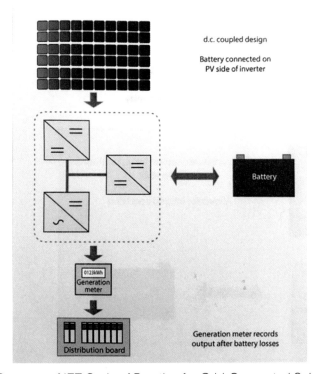

DC coupled system - Courtesy of IET Code of Practice for Grid-Connected Solar Photovoltaic Systems

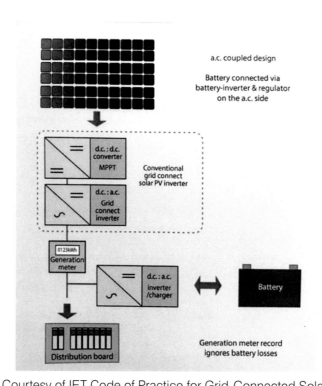

AC coupled system - Courtesy of IET Code of Practice for Grid-Connected Solar Photovoltaic Systems

There are advantages and disadvantages in installing either system. The following table outlines some of these:

AC coupled system	DC coupled system
Equipment • Can use any conventional solar PV inverter • Battery charge-discharge system is wholly separate from the grid-connected PV system • Typically provided by a number of separate and discrete devices • Can be retrofitted to an existing system • Locating the battery away from the PV array and inverter is generally simpler • Provides more choice in battery location • Solar PV inverter needs to be sized to array	• Requires specific solar PV inverter • Battery charge-discharge system is an integral part of the grid-connected PV system • All functions typically provided in a single device. Usually simpler to install • Needs to be installed from the start (or the existing solar PV inverter requires to be replaced or fitted with DC:DC converter) • Battery needs to be located with solar PV inverter • Less choice in battery location or requires longer DC cabling • Solar PV inverter can be significantly smaller
Battery charge efficiency • Increased losses as electricity from PV array gets converted first to AC then back to DC to charge battery	• Reduced battery losses as less conversion stages between PV array and battery.

Key considerations for AC and DC coupled systems table –

Courtesy of BRE Battery energy storage systems with grid-connected solar photovoltaics

For systems which are designed to operate in the event of grid failure, a means to disconnect and isolate the installation from the grid needs to be incorporated into the system. This is shown in the following diagram.

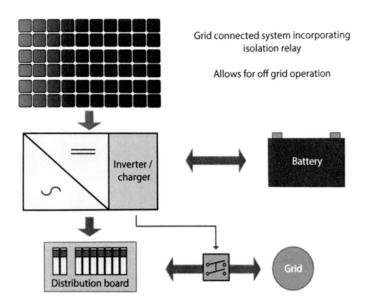

Grid-connected system including isolation relay -

Courtesy of IET Code of Practice for Grid-Connected Solar Photovoltaic Systems

The previous diagram illustrates the entire distribution board/consumer unit being connected to the battery in the event of grid failure. However, this is not a common approach as the inverter rating would need to be appropriate to supply all prospective loads. Therefore, it is typical to separate the loads into essential and non-essential systems, as shown in the next diagram.

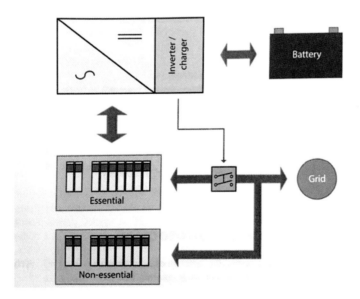

Split system design - Courtesy of IET Code of Practice for Grid-Connected Solar Photovoltaic Systems

Battery system operation

In order to select the appropriate battery system, it has to be understood what and how the system will be used for.

As discussed earlier, a battery storage system can be used in different ways, depending on the requirements of the installed electrical system and the users needs. These could be listed as:

- Basic time-shifting

- Export time-shifting

- Energy security

- Time-shifting and backup

- Peak limiting

In order to understand how time-shifting of generated electrical energy works, it's best to use diagrams as a visual tool to understand the concept.

Daily electrical load profile

This diagram shows how the loads using electrical energy within the installation vary during the day. While shown as a jagged line, the real load use may be considerably more variable, with more pronounced spikes and troughs. Irrespective of these, the given area under this line represents the energy use of the installation in kWh over a period of time.

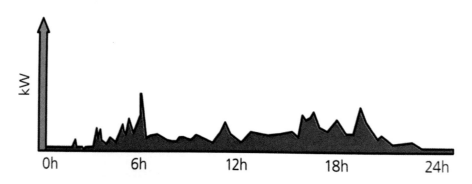

Example of daily electrical load profile -
Courtesy of BRE Battery Energy Storage Systems with Grid-Connected Solar Photovoltaics

Solar generation profile

This diagram shows the generated electrical energy from the PV system during the day. Again, the diagram indicates that the solar irradiation available will take the shape of a bell curve, meaning uninterrupted generation for the entirety of the day. In reality, this curve will have troughs as the irradiance level decreases due to shading by passing clouds and changes in weather.

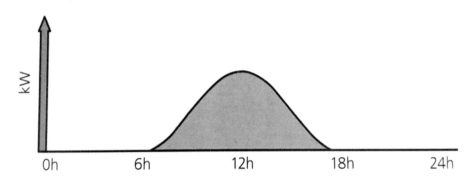

Example of solar generation profile
Courtesy of BRE Battery Energy Storage Systems with Grid-Connected Solar Photovoltaics

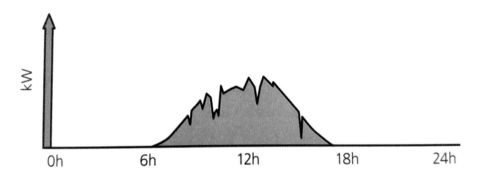

Example of solar generation profile with passing clouds -
Courtesy of BRE Battery Energy Storage Systems with Grid-Connected Solar Photovoltaics

Load and solar overlay

The overlay of the load and solar profiles gives an idea of the generated electrical energy from the PV system which would be available to be diverted to a battery. If a battery storage system was not fitted, the excess available energy would be exported to the grid.

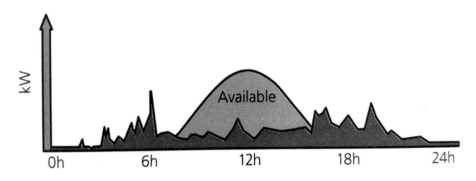

Example of daily electrical load and solar generation profile overlay -
Courtesy of BRE Battery Energy Storage Systems with Grid-Connected Solar Photovoltaics

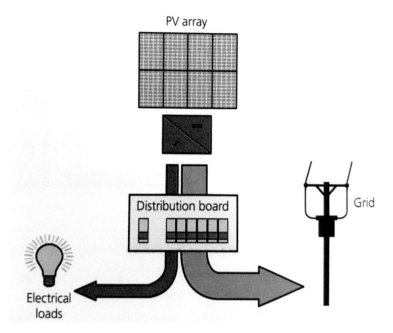

Grid-connected PV system without battery storage -
Courtesy of BRE Battery Energy Storage Systems with Grid-Connected Solar Photovoltaics

Basic time-shifting operation

The concept of time-shifting is to maximise the self-consumption of generated electrical energy from the PV system. with a battery storage system installed, any excess energy generated from the PV system (which isn't being used by local loads) can be diverted to the battery, to be used later that day when the PV system is no longer generating electrical energy.

The process can be broken down into different stages or modes:

- **Mode A**: Loads are supplied from the grid. No output from the PV system and battery is discharged.

- **Mode B**: Output from the PV system supplies the required loads and the excess generated electrical energy is used to charge the battery.

- **Mode C**: Stored electrical energy is used to supply loads until the battery is discharged.

This is an ideal scenario where all the required energy for the loads can be met by either the PV system at the time of generation or by the battery at a time when the PV system is no longer generating. However, variations in load use as well as solar irradiance availability will mean that real system operation is more complex and the system may switch between different modes on multiple occasions during the day.

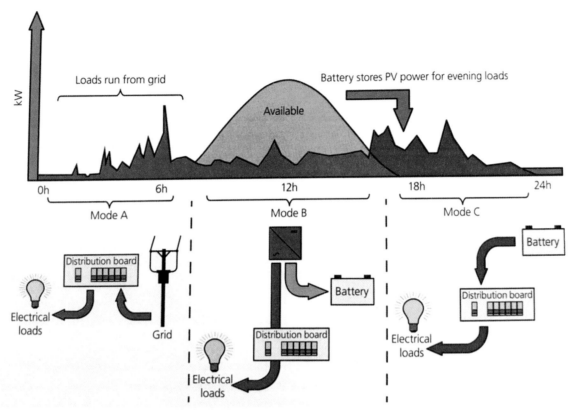

Example of energy storage system operation –
Courtesy of BRE Battery Energy Storage Systems with Grid-Connected Solar Photovoltaics

Battery capacity impact on storage and time-shifting

If the system is primarily being used for time-shifting, the capacity of the battery requires careful consideration.

Where an energy storage system has been installed and the capacity of the battery is suitably sized, all excess generated electrical energy produced by the PV system should be able to be stored, without any being exported to the grid.

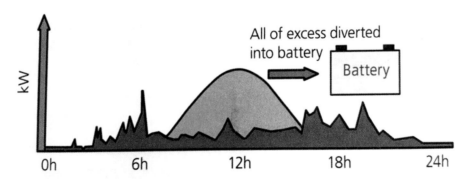

Suitably sized battery storage for excess energy -
Courtesy of BRE Battery Energy Storage Systems with Grid-Connected Solar Photovoltaics

If the battery capacity is too large, it will rarely achieve a full charge and a smaller battery should have been selected. This would probably have reduced the cost of the system.

If the battery capacity is too small, it will not be able to store all the excess generated electrical energy from the PV system. In this instance, any energy not able to be diverted to the battery will be exported to the grid.

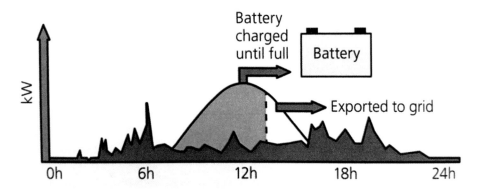

Undersized battery storage for excess energy -
Courtesy of BRE Battery Energy Storage Systems with Grid-Connected Solar Photovoltaics

Export time-shifting

Export time-shifting is an energy storage system which is configured to save all energy generated and then export this at a time of day when it will achieve the best price per unit. For this system to be installed, there has to be an export tariff which changes throughout the day and the system has to be connected through an export meter that includes time-of-day recording.

With the proposed introduction of the Smart Export Guarantee, these types of installations will no doubt become more popular in the near future.

Energy Security

Battery storage systems which are installed and set up to provide energy security are designed to provide an alternative source of supply in the event of grid failure (much like a UPS system). This operating mode is particularly relevant within installations which are subject to frequent power cuts or where the installation has important loads which need to be supplied at all times.

Time-shifting and backup

Where the requirement for both time-shifting and backup supply are required, a battery can be "partitioned" to allow some of its capacity to be used for either activity or multiple batteries can be installed, depending on the requirements of the installation.

Where the battery is partitioned, the system is set up to limit the day-to-day battery DOD. This ensures that at all times, a minimum backup capacity is always available should grid failure occur. The capacity of each partitioned section will depend on the backup requirements of the installation.

Peak limiting

Peak limiting is a term used to describe a system set up to limit the amount of generated electrical energy which is exported by a PV system.

As discussed previously on the course, the DNO is responsible for setting the upper limit of power which a PV system is able to export to the UK national grid system. For small domestic systems, this equates to 16A per phase at 230Vrms, or 3.68kW, as per EREC G98.

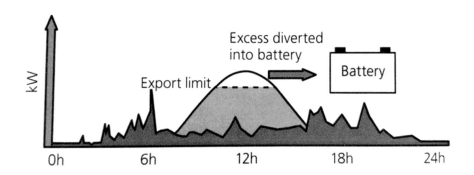

Battery storage in conjunction with an export limit on PV generation -
Courtesy of BRE Battery Energy Storage Systems with Grid-Connected Solar Photovoltaics

Although the maximum power output acceptable to be exported to the grid is 3.68kW, systems with an inverter which is able to exceed this value could be installed where the installation has a certain level of self-consumption though local loading and able to divert any excess after this to the battery storage system or export this to the grid, provided this does not exceed the acceptable limit. The larger inverter would be set up to prevent export above this set limit and ensure the PV system can be safely installed.

All information in this section has been taken from the following documents:

- IET Code of Practice for Grid Connected Solar Photovoltaic Systems

- BRE Battery Energy Storage Systems with Grid-Connected Solar Photovoltaics

Additional information on the design (including component selection and rating) of battery storage systems can be found in the following documents:

- IET Code of Practice for Grid Connected Solar Photovoltaic Systems

- IET Code of Practice for Electrical Energy Storage Systems

- BRE Battery Energy Storage Systems with Grid-Connected Solar Photovoltaics

Appendices

Appendix 01

Abbreviations and Key Terms

PV	Photovoltaic	Light to DC electricity conversion effect
DNO	Distribution Network Operator	List of contacts is available on the PV-UK website
SSEG	Small Scale Embedded Generator	Referred to in ER (Engineering Recommendation) G83/1
PV-UK	British Photovoltaic Association	UK PV trade association
EST	Energy Savings Trust	Grant Scheme Administrator
IV curve	Current-voltage curve	Characteristics PV performance
MPP	Maximum Power Point	Optimal operating point
MPPT	Maximum Power Point Tracking	A function of inverters, to make them operate most efficiently
VOC	Open-Circuit Voltage	No load, maximum voltage, zero current – one end of IV curve
Vmp or Vmpp	Maximum Power (Point) Voltage	Voltage of optimal operation
ISC	Short Circuit Current	Full load, zero voltage, maximum current – other end of IV curve
Imp or Impp	Maximum Power (Point) Current	Current of optimal operation
STC	Standard Test Conditions	Temperature 25°C, irradiance 1000 wm, air mass 1.5 (Spectrum)
NOC	Nominal Operating Conditions	Expected average operating conditions
a-Si	Amorphous Silicon	Thin film PV material, brown in colour, discrete 'strips'
c-Si	Crystalline Silicon	Crystalline PV material, black (or blue and faceted for multi-), discrete cells
Wp	Watt-peak	Power rating PV at STC, 1000 Wp = 1kWp
AONB	Area of Outstanding Natural Beauty	Planning permission required for PV installation
SSSI	Site of Special Scientific Interest	Planning permission required for PV installation
CDM	Construction (Design and Management) Regulations 1994	Only apply to large installations for a non-domestic client
COSHH	Control of Substances Hazardous to Health	Regulation regarding handling and storage of toxic materials
HSE	Health and Safety Executive	Supplies information on safety e.g. working at height
BIPV	Building Integrated PV	PV installed within the building envelope e.g. roof tiles, façades
Abbreviations for reference		
IEC	International Electrotechnical Committee	e.g. PV module standards IEC 61215 (c-Si) and IEC 61646 (a-Si)
ENA	Energy Networks Association	Supplies copies of Engineering Recommendations e.g. G83/1 and G59/1
PPG22/	Planning Policy Guidance 22/	This document refers to PV and planning
PPS22	Planning Policy Statement 22	G83/1 and G59/1
CT	Current Transformer	Coil for measuring current flowing through conductor. Used by kWh meters

Appendix 02

One Commissioning Pro-forma per installation is to be submitted to the DNO.

Form B: Installation Document for connection under G98
Please complete and provide this document for each premises, once **Micro-generator** installation is complete.

To	ABC electricity distribution	**DNO**
99 West St, Imaginary Town, ZZ99 9AA		abced@wxyz.com

Customer Details:

Customer (name)	
Address	
Post Code	
Contact person (if different from Customer)	
Telephone number	
E-mail address	
Customer signature	

Installer Details:

Installer	
Accreditation / Qualification	
Address	
Post Code	
Contact person	
Telephone Number	
E-mail address	
Installer signature	

Installation details

Address	
Post Code	
MPAN(s)	
Location within **Customer's Installation**	
Location of Lockable Isolation Switch	

Details of Micro-generators. Use a separate line for new and existing installations and for different technology type. Use PH 1 column for single phase supply.

Manufacturer				Micro-generator Registered Capacity in kW					
	Date of Installation	Technology Type / Primary Energy Source please enter code from table below	**Manufacturer's** Ref No (this number should be registered on the ENA **Type Test Verification** Report Register as Product ID)	3-Phase Units	Single Phase Units				Power Factor
						PH1	PH2	PH3	

Declaration – to be completed by Installer for Micro-generators Tested to EREC G98

I declare that the relevant **Micro-generator**s and the installation which together form a **Micro-generating Plant** within the scope of EREC G98 at the above address, conform to the requirements of EREC G98. This declaration of compliance is confined to **Micro-generating Plant** tested to EREC G98 or EREC G83 as applicable at the time of commissioning.

Signature:	Date:

Primary Energy Source	Code	Primary Energy Source	Code
Solar PV	1	Wind	2
Hydro (run of river)	3	Hydro (reservoir)	4
Biomass	5	Other Renewable	6
Fossil gas	7	Waste	8
Fossil coal gas	9	Fossil oil	10
Fossil oil shale	11	Fossil peat	12
Geothermal	13	Fossil brown coal/lignite	14
Fossil hard coal	15	Hydro pumped storage	16
Marine	17	Nuclear	18
Offshore wind	19	Other	20
Other – battery storage	21	Other – storage - not battery	22

The information requested herein complies with the requirements of Engineering Recommendation of the current edition G98.

Appendix 03

PV Array Test Report		Initial Verification
		Periodic Verification
Installation address		Reference
		Date
Description of work under test		Inspector
		Test instruments

String		1	2	3	4		n
Array	Module						
	Quantity						
Array parameters (as specified)	Voc (stc)						
	Ioc (stc)						
String over-current protective device	Type						
	Rating (A)						
	DC Rating (V)						
	Capacity (kA)						
String wiring	Type						
	Phase (mm^2)						
	Earth (mm^2)						
String test	Voc (V)						
	Isc (A)						
	Irradiance						
Polarity check							
Array insulation resistance	Test Voltage (V)						
	Pos - Earth (MΩ)						
	Neg - Earth (MΩ)						
Earth Continuity (where fitted)							
Array Isolator	Rating (A)						
	Rating (V)						
	Location						
	Functional Check						
Inverter	Make and model						
	Serial number						
	Functioning OK						
Loss of mains test							
Comments							

DOMESTIC PHOTOVOLTAIC (PV) ELECTRICAL INSTALLATION (For a single dwelling)
SCHEDULE OF INSPECTIONS
☐ All data entry boxes must be completed. To provide a positive indication that an inspection or test has been carried out, insert either a 'Yes' or a tick. Where an inspection or a test is not relevant to the installation, insert 'N/A' meaning 'Not Applicable'.
Schedule of Inspection – PV System

DC system – General

The entire system has been inspected to the requirements of IEC 60364-6 and an inspection report to meet the requirements of IEC 60364-6 is attached.

☐ The DC system has been designed, specified and installed to the requirements of IEC 60364 and IEC 62548:2016.

☐ The maximum PV array voltage is suitable for the array location.

☐ All system components and mounting structures have been selected and erected to withstand the expected external influences such as wind, snow, temperature and corrosion.

☐ Roof fixings and cable entries are weatherproof (where applicable).

DC system – Protection against electric shock

☐ Protective measure provided by extra low voltage (SELV/PELV)

☐ Protection by use of class II or equivalent insulation adopted on the DC side.

☐ PV string and array cables have been selected and erected so as to minimise the risk of earth faults and short circuits. Typically achieved using cables with protective and reinforced insulation (often termed "double insulation").

For systems where the inverter(s) can produce a DC back-feed into the PV array circuits:

☐ Any back-feed current is lower than both the module maximum fuse rating and the string cable ampere rating.

DC system – Earthing and bonding arrangements

Where the PV system includes functional earthing of one of the DC conductors:

☐ The functional earthing connection has been specified and installed to the requirements of IEC 62548:2016.

Where a PV system has a direct connection to earth on the DC side:

☐ A functional earth fault interrupter is provided to the requirements of IEC 62548:2016.

☐ Array frame bonding arrangements have been specified and installed to the requirements of IEC 62548:2016.

Where protective earthing and/or equipotential bonding conductors are installed:

☐ They are parallel to, and bundled with, the DC cables.

DOMESTIC PHOTOVOLTAIC (PV) ELECTRICAL INSTALLATION (For a single dwelling (Continued))
Schedule of Inspection – PV System (Continued)

DC system – Protection against the effects of insulation faults

☐ Galvanic separation in place inside the inverter or on the AC side.

☐ Functional earthing of any DC conductor

☐ PV Array Earth Insulation Resistance detection and alarm system installed – to the requirements of IEC 62548:2016.

☐ PV Array Earth Residual Current Monitoring detection and alarm system is installed – to the requirements of IEC 62548:2016

DC system – Protection against overload

For systems without string overcurrent protective device:

☐ IMOD_MAX_OCPR (the module maximum series fuse rating) is greater than the possible reverse current;

☐ String cables are sized to accommodate the maximum combined fault current from parallel strings.

For systems with string overcurrent protective device:

☐ String overcurrent protective devices are fitted and correctly specified to the requirements of IEC 62548:2016.

For systems with array/sub-array overcurrent protective device:

☐ Overcurrent protective devices are fitted and correctly specified to the requirements of IEC 62548:2016.

DC system – Protection against the effects of lightning and overvoltage

☐ To minimise voltages induced by lightning, the area of all wiring loops has been kept as small as possible.

☐ Measures are in place to protect long cables (e.g. screening or the use of SPDs)

☐ Where SPDs are fitted, they have been installed to the requirement of IEC 62548:2016.

DC system – Selection and erection of electrical equipment

☐ The PV modules are rated for the maximum possible DC system voltage.

☐ All DC components are rated for continuous operation at DC and at the maximum possible DC system voltage and current as defined in IEC 62548:2016.

☐ Wiring systems have been selected and erected to withstand the expected external influences such as wind, ice formation, temperature, UV and solar radiation.

☐ Means of isolation and disconnection have been provided for the PV array strings and PV sub-arrays – to the requirements of IEC 62548:2016

☐ A DC switch disconnector is fitted to the DC side of the inverter to the requirements of IEC 62548:2016.

DOMESTIC PHOTOVOLTAIC (PV) ELECTRICAL INSTALLATION (For a single dwelling (Continued))

Schedule of Inspection – PV System

☐ Plug and socket connectors mated together are of the same type and from the same manufacturer and comply with the requirements of IEC 62548:2016.

AC System

☐ A means of isolating the inverter has been provided on the AC side.

☐ All isolation and switching devices have been connected such that PV installation is wired to the "load" side and the public supply to the "source" side.

☐ The inverter operational parameters have been programmed to local regulations.

☐ Where an RCD is installed to the AC circuit feeding an inverter, the RCD type has been verified to ensure it has been selected according to the requirements of IEC 63548:2016.

Labelling and identification

☐ All circuits, protective devices, switches and terminals suitably labelled to the requirements of IEC 60364 and IEC 62548:2016.

☐ All DC junction boxes (PV generator and PV array boxes) carry a warning label indicating that active parts inside the boxes are fed from a PV array and may still be live after isolation from the PV inverter and public supply.

☐ Means of isolation on the AC side is clearly labelled.

☐ If blocking diodes are fitted, their reverse voltage rating is at least 2 x VOC (stc) of the PV string in which they are fitted (see IEC 62548:2016.

DOMESTIC PHOTOVOLTAIC (PV) ELECTRICAL INSTALLATION (For a single dwelling (Continued))

Schedule of Inspection – PV System

☐ Dual supply warning labels are fitted at point of interconnection.

☐ A single line wiring diagram is displayed on site.

☐ Installer details are displayed on site.

☐ Shutdown procedures are displayed on site.

☐ Emergency procedures are displayed on site.

☐ All signs and labels are suitable fixed and durable.

INSPECTED BY

Signature		Position	
Name (CAPITALS)		Date Tested	
Schedule of Test Results Certificate number			